ANCHORING

STEVEN HOLL

SELECTED PROJECTS 1975–1988

PRINCETON ARCHITECTURAL PRESS

Princeton Architectural Press
37 East Seventh Street
New York, NY 10003
212-995-9620
ISBN 0-910413-19-3

Published in Great Britain by
Butterworth Architecture
an imprint of Butterworth Scientific
Part of Reed International PLC
ISBN 0408 50046 8

92 91 90 89   5 4 3 2 1
Project editor: Elizabeth Short
Copy editor: Ann Urban
Book design: Kevin Lippert
Production: Clare Jacobson
Special thanks to Stephen Cassell, Sheila Cohen,
Marsha Davis, Tim Tice, and Amy Weisser.

For Myron & Helen

CONTENTS

ACKNOWLEDGMENTS. In Seattle I had the good fortune to study under Professor Hermann Pundt, who led his students with focused passion through the works of Schinkel to Sullivan and Wright. Professor Pundt's lasting admonishment was: "Travel for the direct experience of architecture; it is the only way to learn. Photographs cannot be trusted." In those years I learned the principles of architecture, declarations for clarity and simplicity. It is no wonder that the book *Complexity and Contradiction,* handed to me in 1967 by a professor at the University of Washington, left me skeptical and unmoved.

When I was given an opportunity to study in Rome, Professor Astra Zarina revealed to me a life-breath of cultural dimensions that cannot be separated from architecture.

Internship years spent in San Francisco alongside the ever-obsessive William Stout, the energetic Mark Mack, and Stanley Saitowitz were filled with dialogue. The challenge of study at The Architectural Association in London, with colleagues like Zaha Hadid and Rem Koolhaus, was encircled with obsessive visits to sites of modern architecture in Europe. New York has been a difficult but exhilarating city in which Andrew McNair and Lebbeus Woods have been supportive friends, and Ken Frampton an important critic. Years of living in a half-empty, cold-water department store with two windows overlooking a cemetery on 21st Street strengthened the spirit. Manhattan would never have been a home for me without the support of my brother, James, a painter and sculptor, whose dedication to his art continues regardless of the endless barriers this city puts in front of artists of integrity.

Lastly, this book would not be a reality without the dedicated effort of Princeton Architectural Press, who produced it with the love I hope to instill in works of architecture.

—Steven Holl, Manchester, WA, December, 1988

PUBLISHER'S FOREWORD
Kevin Lippert

Even those who know the work of Steven Holl may find it surprising that he has chosen "Anchoring"—the relationship of building to site—as the theme of this first book on his architecture. For at first, or even second, glance, Holl's architecture seems to be about many things other than site.

In its laconic simplicity, his work seems initially to be about the language of architecture, not in the allusive sense used by postmodernists nor in the paradigmatic sense used by so-called "deconstructivists," but at the level of essences, of tropes and morphes—what Holl calls the "proto-elements" of architecture. The stark facade of the Rosen Pool House confronts the viewer with its *openings,* which are only nominally differentiated into *door* and *window.* Eventually, we are offered *sill, pane, cornice,* and *roof*—nothing more—but even with this almost pre-syllabic vocabulary, the Pool House remains one of Holl's richest and most eloquent works. This spareness has caused many to call him a neo-modernist, but Holl does not—as did Le Corbusier by invoking the imagery of aircraft

and boats, for example—use the vocabulary of modernism to identify a technological agenda, nor to recall nostalgically an architectural style. Holl is a modernist only in a reductive sense, in the way that early modernists stripped the column down to its columnar essence. For Holl, this reduction is linked to an integrity of construction and expression and rejection of ornamental obfuscation, rather than any complex external theory.

Holl's work also seems to be about *techne* or craft, about the delight in making and discovering details and materials. Mies's dictum "God is in the details" holds true equally for Holl. If his architecture stands silent, his sandblasted glass panes, lighting fixtures, cabinetry, artifacts, and furniture whisper, all the more clearly because of their austere frame. "Ornament is spare," writes Holl, "and directly related to the craft of working the materials in which it occurs." It is also emblematic; the etched-glass details of the Guardian Safe Depository, for example, contain Kepler's diagram of 1596 comparing the five regular solids to the

(then) six planets, a key to the organization of this now-destroyed building. The (literally) bulging window of the Giada showroom suggests the compression of this minute space. The masterfully-applied, sensually-smooth plaster of the MoMA Tower Apartment corresponds to the X-, Y-, and Z-axes of the Manhattan grid.

Holl's architecture is also about proportion and mathematics. The Golden Section figures in his candlesticks as it does in his elevations for the Telescope House. Vitruvius warns that without proportion there can be no design, and Holl's attention to this admonishment not only links his work to a Classical/Renaissance tradition, but establishes an underlying—albeit scalable and often invisible—frame for his entire oeuvre. This adherence to geometric rigor satisfies, in Holl's mind, a spiritual need in architecture that transcends rudimentary function.

The vernacular also informs Holl's work. Born in Washington State, he brings an interest in the timber structures of the Pacific Northwest, a celebration of the "carpenter architect." His research for the seminal *Pamphlet Architecture* series often dealt with the vernacular. *Urban and Rural House Types, The Alphabetical City,* and *Hybrid Buildings* (in conjunction with Joseph Fenton) reduced, categorized, and catalogued plantypes, volumetrics, and functions. There is a fine line between Holl's analytic diagrams and many of his early projects, each an "ongoing search for elements, or ABCs." The vernacular, for Holl, if not unknowingly then silently expresses values—an adherence to type and geometry—often absent in "high architecture."

Unfashionable as it may be today, there is also a social text in Holl's work. Although most overt in the programs of his earliest projects—Manila Housing and the Bronx Gymnasium Bridge, for example—even in recent projects, such as the Seaside Building and Milan Project, there is always an underlying concern about how people live, work, and play in his spaces. Holl's is not a naive social utopianism, but a concern for the *individual,* for the poetics of life: contemplation and withdrawal, stimulation and animation, private and public.

Fundamentally, however, Holl's architecture is about phenomenology. In *The Alphabetical City,* Holl warns that "today there is much building, and almost no architecture." For Holl, architecture without idea—without a consciousness of the experience of architecture, its materials, light, shadow, color, scale, and proportion—is only building. His reading of Husserl and Heidegger focuses on the experiential and tactile dimensions of architecture. His later work takes this beyond questions of detail and materials to spatial perception and procession, an almost filmic sensibility.

It is here that Holl arrives at anchoring. More than the physical siting of a building, anchoring involves both a conceptual rooting and an experiential one. The Berkowitz house is anchored by its literary reference to a beached whale in Moby Dick; the Milan Triennale project is anchored by its complex perceptual organization. Anchoring also involves an almost metaphysical reversal: the site is then modified by the very piece of architecture conceived for it. The tools that Holl uses—his spare language, proportion, attention to detail, and research of the vernacular—are only means to establish, develop, and enhance this phenomenological linkage between building and site.

Writing in *Urban and Rural House Types,* Holl could have been summarizing his own work: "A spirit of geometry, a sense of independent thought, a consistent measure and preparation of detail, and an overall coherence." What makes Steven Holl one of the most interesting and important architects practicing today is not only the success of his many projects and his contribution to architectural discourse, but the fact that he has succeeded with an almost disarming integrity. Where many of his colleagues rush toward commercial success, Holl is suspicious of it: it risks compromise. He has also stayed at arms-length from much of the Eastcoast intellectual debate, preferring the more modest and, at times, deliberately a-theoretical *Pamphlet Architecture* as his forum. That an architect can, in what Holl calls "this time of painted cardboard," succeed without compromise or the blessing of a theoretical godfather should be inspiration for other architects of his generation and those to come.

ANCHORING
Steven Holl

Writing's relation to architecture affords only an uncertain mirror to be held up to evidence; it is rather in a wordless silence that we have the best chance to stumble into that zone comprised of space, light, and matter that is architecture. Although they fall short of architectural evidence, words present a premise. The work is forced to carry over when words themselves cannot. Words are arrows pointing in the right directions; taken together they form a map of architectural intentions.

Here, then, are some excerpted thoughts that have, over the past ten years, acted as catalysts for the projects that follow.

ANCHORING. Architecture is bound to situation. Unlike music, painting, sculpture, film, and literature, a construction (non-mobile) is intertwined with the experience of a place. The site of a building is more than a mere ingredient in its conception. It is its physical and metaphysical foundation.

The resolution of the functional aspects of site and building, the vistas, sun angles, circulation, and access, are the "physics" that demand the "metaphysics" of architecture. Through a link, an extended motive, a building is more than something merely fashioned for the site.

Building transcends physical and functional requirements by fusing with a place, by gathering the meaning of a situation. Architecture does not so much intrude on a landscape as it serves to explain it. Illumination of a site is not a simplistic replication of its "context"; to reveal an aspect of a place may not confirm its "appearance." Hence the habitual ways of seeing may well be interrupted.

Architecture and site should have an experiential connection, a metaphysical link, a poetic link.

When a work of architecture successfully fuses a building and situation, a third condition emerges. In this third entity, denotation and connotation merge; expression is linked to idea which is joined to site. The suggestive and implicit are manifold aspects of an intention.

A building has one site. In this one situation, its intentions are collected. Building and site have been interdependent since the beginning of Architecture. In the past, this connection was manifest without conscious intention through the use of local materials and craft, and by an association of the landscape with events of history and myth. Today the link between site and architecture must be found in new ways, which are part of a constructive transformation in modern life.

Ideas cultivated from the first perception of the site, meditations upon initial thoughts, or a reconsideration of existing topography can become the framework for invention. This mode of invention is focused through a relative space, as distinct from universal space. It is in a bounded domain. Architecture is an extension; a modification establishing absolute meanings relative to a place. Even when a new work is an inversion of inherent conditions, its order attempts to embody an aspect, or illuminate a specific meaning distinct from generalities of abstract space. An ideal exists in the specific; an absolute in the relative.

Standing in the courtyard of the Nunnery in Uxmal, time is transparent, function unknown. The path of the sun is perfectly ordered with the architecture. The framed views align with the distant hills. Descending through the ball court, ascending the "House of Turtles," and looking again toward the great courtyard—the experience trancends architectural beauty. Architecture and site are phenomenologically linked.

At Louis Kahn's Salk Institute, there is a time of day when the sun, reflecting on the ocean, merges with light reflecting on the rivulet of water in the trough bisecting the central court. Ocean and

Uxmal: View from "House of Turtles."

courtyard are fused by the phenomenon of sunlight reflecting on water. Architecture and nature are joined in a metaphysics of place.

Across a vast, fecund valley in Oregon, an ir-regular form clings to the edge of the Benedictine Monastery on Mt. Angel. Approached from the gar-den of the hilltop cloister, it appears as a low one-story building of modest consequence. Once in-side, it unfolds in a burst of space splayed outward and downward, freely engaged in the rolling pano-rama of earth and sky. Aalto completed the edge of the monastic plateau and created a serene cas-cade of space for study and contemplation. The qualities of the architecture are fused with the qualities and meaning of its situation.

The grand shrines of Ise, Japan are recon-structed every twenty years on adjacent sites; each temple has two sites. Since 4 B.C., this religious act has had a mysterious power most manifest in the vacant site with its stone pads ready to receive the adjacent temple according to the next twenty-year cycle. Time and site are further engaged in the Sakaki—the paper ornaments hanging on the

gates and fences that are replaced fresh every ten days.

Adalberto Libera's Malaparte residence in Capri stands as a mysterious example of order in space, light, and time. Its simple walls merge with the rock and cliffs and rise from the Mediterranean like a strange platform offering itself to the sun. Without style, almost without identifiable eleva-tions, it connects with the site by jumping over time.

IDEA AND PHENOMENA. The essence of a work of architecture is an organic link between concept and form. Pieces cannot be subtracted or added without upsetting fundamental properties. A con-cept, whether a rationally explicit statement or a subjective demonstration, establishes an order, a field of inquiry, a limited principle.

Within the phenomena of experience in a built construction, the organizing idea is a hidden thread connecting disparate parts with exact intention. Al-though the experience of semi-transparent planes of glass defining a space with a glow of light pre-sents a sensory experience irreduceable to a

stated concept, this inexpression is not a gap be-tween concept and phenomena, but the range or field where various conclusions intersect.

The intertwining of idea and phenomena oc-curs when a building is realized. Before beginning, architecture's metaphysical skeleton of time, light, space, and matter remain unordered. Modes of composition are open: line, plane, volume, and proportion await activation. When site, culture, and program are given, an order, an idea may be formed. Yet the idea is only conception.

The transparency of a membrane, the chalky dullness of a wall, the glossy reflection of opaque glass, and a beam of sunlight intermesh in recipro-cal relationships that form the particular ex-perience of a place. Materials interlocking with the perceiver's senses provide the detail that moves us beyond acute sight to tactility. From linearity, con-cavity, and transparency to hardness, elasticity, and dampness, the haptic realm opens.

An architecture of matter and tactility aims for a "poetics of revealing" (Martin Heidegger), which re-quires an inspiration of joinery. Detail, this poetics of revealing, interplays intimate scaled dissonance with large scale consonance. The vertical patience of a massive wall is interrupted by a solitary and miniature cage of clarity, at once giving scale and revealing material and matter.

Similarly, the spatial experience of parallax, or perspective warp, while moving through overlapping spaces defined by solids and cavities opens the phenomena of spatial fields. The experience of space from a point of view that is in perspective presents a coupling of the external space of the horizon and the optic point from the body. Eye sockets become a kind of architectural position grounded in a phenomena of spatial experience that must be reconciled with the concept and its absence of experiential spatiality.

An infinite number of perspectives projected from an infinite number of viewpoints could be said to make up the spatial field of the phenomena of a work of architecture.

Space remains in oblivion without light. Light's shadow and shade, its different sources, its opacity, transparency, translucency, and conditions of reflection and refraction intertwine to define or redefine space. Light subjects space to uncertainty, forming a kind of tentative bridge through fields of experience. What a pool of yellow light does to a simple bare volume or what a paraboloid of shadow does to a bone white wall presents us with a psychological and transcendant realm of the phenomena of architecture.

If we consider the order (the idea) to be the outer perception and the phenomena (the experience) to be the inner perception, then in a physical construction, outer perception and inner perception are intertwined. From this position experiential phenomena are the material for a kind of reasoning that joins concept and sensation. The objective is unified with the subjective. Outer perception (of the intellect) and inner perception (of the senses) are synthesized in an ordering of space, light, and material.

Architectural thought is the working through of phenomena initiated by idea. By "making" we realize idea is only a seed for extension in phenomena. Sensations of experience become a kind of reasoning distinct to the making of architecture. Whether reflecting on the unity of concept and sensation or the intertwining of idea and phenomena, the hope is to unite intellect and feeling, precision with soul.

PROTO-ELEMENTS OF ARCHITECTURE (AN OPEN LANGUAGE). The open vocabulary of

modern architecture may be extended by any compositional element, form, method, or geometry. A situation immediately sets limits. A chosen ordering concept and chosen materials begin the effort to extract the nature of the work. Prior to site, even prior to culture, a tangible vocabulary of the elements of architecture remains open. Here is a beautiful potential: proto-elements of architecture.

Proto-elements: possible combinations of lines, planes, and volumes in space remain disconnected, trans-historical, and trans-cultural. They float about in a zero-ground of form without gravity but are precursors of a concrete architectonic form. There are elements that are transcultural and transtemporal, common to the ancient architecture of Kyoto and of Rome. These elements are fundamental geometric precepts common to ancient Egypt and high Gothic, to twentieth-century rationalism and expressionism.

Lines: stems of grass, twigs, cracks in mud, cracks in ice, veins in a leaf, woodgrain, nodal lines, spiderwebs, hair, ripples in sand . . . The astonishing Gothic stone tracery of King's College Chapel, of Westminster Abbey, or of Gloucester Cathedral. The steel linearity of Paxton's Crystal Palace . . .

Malaparte House by A. Libera, Capri, Italy 1938.

Wing of a fly.

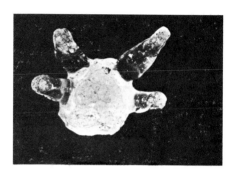

Left: Hailstone that fell at Sydney, Australia
on 3 January, 1971.

Planes: ribbons of seaweed, palm leaves, cabbage, sediments, stone, elephant ears, sheets of water, wings, feathers, papyrus . . . The planar wall architecture of ancient Egypt; the temple of Luxor. The wonderful superimposed lyrical planarity of Terragni's Casa Giuliani-Frigerio or of Rietveld's Schroder House.

Volumes: nautilus shells, pumpkins, watermelon, tree trunks, icebergs, endomorph crystals, cactus, planets . . . The volumetric intensities of Roman architecture, the stone drums, the pure pyramid of Cestius or the Romanesque interior volumes of St. Front at Periguex.

An open language, an extension of the field of architecture is analogous to the range of composition in modern music. As a student of music might study the widest variations and structures in composition, so the student of architecture must cultivate an appetite for composition that is other than a habitual way of seeing. The combination of tones in a harmonic unit or the dissonance that reflects another side of consonance have architectural parallels. If music no longer depends on adherance to a major-minor system of values or a system of classical tonality, our musical range is extended. In the study of the composition of architecture we may likewise seek to extend its range but remain open to the inevitable limits that define it with each circumstance and site.

IDEOLOGY VS. IDEA. General theories of architecture are constrained by a central problem; that is to say, if a particular theory is true, then all other theories are false. Pluralism, on the other hand, leads to an empirical architecture. A third direction, as potentially resilient as it is definite, is the adoption of a limited concept. Time, culture, programmatic circumstance, and site are specific factors from which an organizing idea can be formed. A specific concept may be developed as a precise order, irrespective of the universal claims of any particular ideology.

A theory of architecture that leads to a system for thinking about and making buildings has, at its base, a series of fixed ideas constituting an ideology. The ideology is evident in each project that is consistent with the general theory. By contrast, an architecture based on a limited concept begins with dissimilarity and variation. It illuminates the singularity of a specific situation.

Principles of proportion or deliberation on rhythm and numbers are not invalidated by beginning with a "limited" concept. Abstract principles of architectural composition take a subordinate position within the organizing idea. The "universal-to-specific" order is inverted to become "specific-to-universal."

The critic will observe that this strategy of inversion may become an ideology in itself. This is not the intention here, but even so, this would be an ideology forever changing, a black swan theory, mutable and unpredictable. This would be an ideology denying the homogeneity of the accepted by celebrating the extraordinary, parallel to nature's diversity. If it is a theory, it is a theory that allows for an architecture of strange and mysterious beginnings, with the hope of original and unique meaning in each place. Its aim is variation, precision, and a celebration of the as-yet-unknown.

"The aspects of things that are most important for us are hidden because of their simplicity and familiarity."

—L. Wittgenstein

Above: Site plan showing scope of proposal.
Right: Existing conditions.

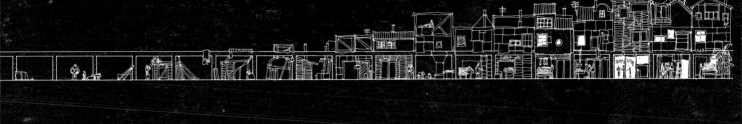

MANILA HOUSING The Philippines 1975–76. This proposal for an international competition for housing in the squatter settlements in Daga Dagatan, Manila focuses the personal energy of each family by providing permanent tenure on a plot of land. The line defining public and private space is formed by a concrete arcade that sets the layout of the streets and the hierarchy of open spaces. With utility services in place, inhabitants build according to their imagination and determination, creating spontaneous house plans. The plan's ordered system of public spaces offers the greatest degree of individual flexibility. Houses reflect the owner's response to *silong* (flooding), winds, sun, and views. With permanent tenure, a personal investment in craft and construction can develop over time.

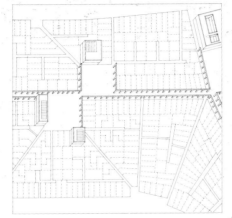

Left: Initial construction
Above: Spontaneous house plans.

An absolute minimum proposal:
definition of the public/private line,
permanent tenure and utilities.

15

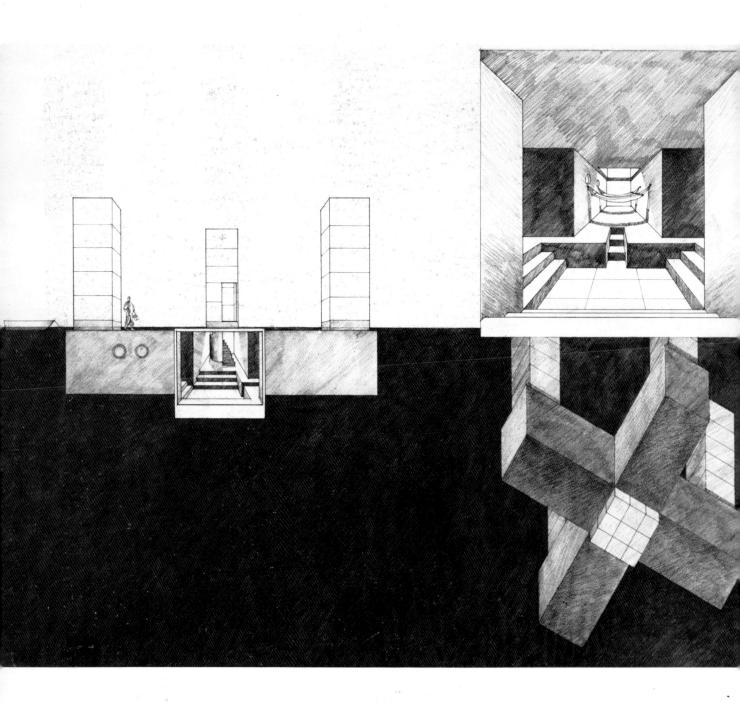

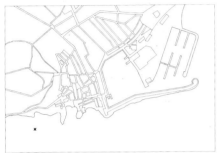

SOKOLOV RETREAT St. Tropez, France 1976.
The noise and confusion of vacation crowds in the harbor of St. Tropez suggested the need for a retreat from a vacation house. The retreat is easily accessible from the client's waterfront house. Silence and solitude are primary concerns.

The retreat is underwater, anchored in front of the existing house at the edge of the harbor. Floating four centimeters below the surface of the water, the chamber is invisible except for the hollow glass block towers for light and air. The towers extend upwards to guard against waves and to increase

air circulation via the principle of the chimney draft.

The effort required for entry contributes to the sensation of a retreat: one must row from the mainland, secure the rowboat, and, with shoes off and trousers rolled, cross the submerged deck to the tower containing the entry stair.

The area of the plan stretches into a cruciform, like a catamaran leaning in two directions, to minimize rocking. Within the plan, one can retreat toward the ends to the hammocks or sit in the central meeting area, which has a glass bottom. The hollow glass block towers are at the endpoints of

the plan for the best distribution of light and air. One tower is equipped with a ladder allowing eccentric guests the opportunity to dive off into the bay.

The structure is a resin-coated ferroconcrete, a thin shell construction with layered wire mesh. Automatic sump pump and adjustable ballast in the double bottom maintain flotation and protect against overloading and listing. The towers are steel-secured glass block with silicone joints and acrylic rain flaps. Floors and walls are polished pigmented concrete. The hammocks are uncolored canvas.

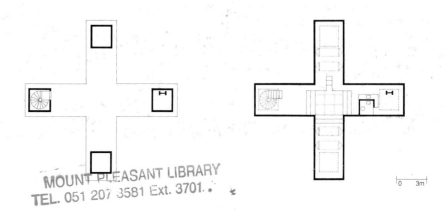

0   3m

17

STATE CAPITOL BUILDING St. Paul, Minnesota
1976. The strongest single influence in the formation of Minnesota goes back 15,000 years to the continental glaciers that withdrew toward the Arctic in a slow but cataclysmic motion, leaving pitted moraines, watery cuts, and a morass of lakes. The massive Pleistocene sheets of ice engraved deeply the rolling landscape where waters sunk to the recessed levels and remained. Irregular deposits of till, ice block basins, and outwash plains along preglacial valleys are characteristic of an inventory of the origin of the lake basins in Minnesota, the "Land of 10,000 Lakes."

The competition program for the State Capitol consolidates a museum for collecting and preserving the records of the past with governing functions in a subterranean structure.

This proposal is conceived as a compressed allegorical account of the history of Minnesota. The exaltation of history is confined to the Great Hall, which contains formal and solemn functions. Beneath a glacial cover of glass block panels, prismatically diffused light reaches the upper loggia and its dark-green plants—specially selected to recall vegetation following glacial recessions. The arcaded perimeter of the great hall is ochre-colored concrete, forming a fossil impression of the first State Capitol (circa 1848). The compressed/extended homage is not a literal reconstruction but an impression inside-out. The cavities left in these in-side-out elevations recall the sparse details and elegant proportions of the original colonial structure. Stairways to the main floor, which appear to be pressed into the ochre concrete, are of contrasting white marble. The upper loggia of the legislative facilities retains a dignified character paved in St. Cloud granite with inside surfaces trimmed in the dark blue and gold of the state flag. The main floor includes metaphorical accounts of the Carver's Cave, where in 1767 native Indian tribes conferred with explorers (the first council meetings in the Capitol City). Other important events are recorded in colored wall drawings and petroglyphs inside the lower arcade. These records of human episodes lie appropriately beneath the small portion of the

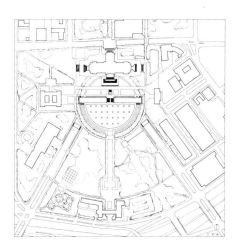

building exposed above, whose frosted glass surface is partially enveloped in water during summer, providing a quiet activity for the shallow water court with the freshness of watered gardens.

The organization of the solemn functions of the scheme is succinct and categorical. History is clearly arranged according to human law, an ordered succession of causes and effects. These logical rationales are united along a poetic reaction, where a sense of history is in a tumultuous dynamic intersection; a glacial reverie that stands as a silent fable of the history of Minnesota.

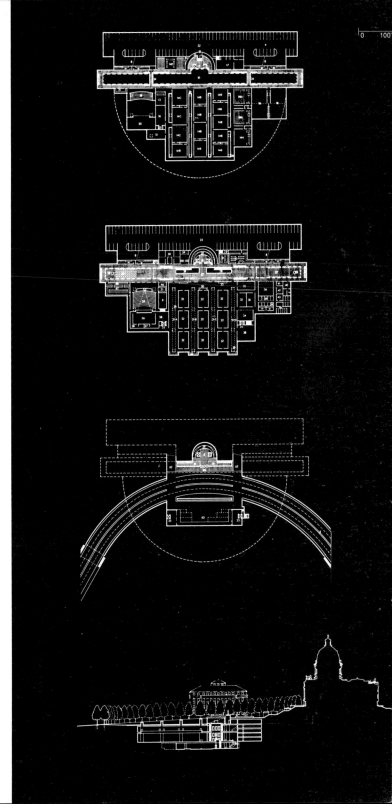

GYMNASIUM-BRIDGE South Bronx, New York 1977. Penn Central's South Bronx railroad yards have fallen into disuse. The site is boxed in by bridges and elevated highways with a ceiling formed by the flight patterns of planes landing and taking off from La Guardia airport. The program called for "ideas or strategies that would yield incremental benefits for the immediate neighborhood." The only explicit requirement is a pedestrian bridge from the South Bronx to the park on Randall's Island. The bridge "must not assume a form that would jeopardize the future development of the site for commercial or industrial purposes, including deep water ship movement in the canal." The immediate neighborhood of the South Bronx with a population of approximately 400,000 has unemployment of 45% to 50%.

The Gymnasium-Bridge is a hybrid building synthesized as a special strategy for generating positive economic and physical effects. The Gymnasium-Bridge condenses the activities of meeting, physical recreation, and work into one structure that simultaneously forms a bridge from the community to the park on Randall's Island.

Along the bridge, community members participate in competitive sports and physical activities organized according to a normal work day with wages provided by a branch of the Urban Jobs Corp or a reconstituted WPA. While earning enough money to become economically stable, community members gain physical and moral strength and develop a sense of community spirit. The bridge becomes a vehicle from which destitute persons can reenter society, become accustomed to a normal work day, and help gain the strength to develop their full individual potential.

The form of the architecture is a series of bridges over bridges. The small entrance bridges at each end of the main span preserve the view down Brook Street to the canal, and from Randall's Island up Brook Street. The main span is aligned with this axis and is crossed by a fourth and highest bridge. In water rather than over water, this bridge acts as a structural pivot from which the turnbridge portion of the main span rotates to allow future ship passage in the waterway. At its base are floats for competition rowboats, which are an extension of the activities and payroll of the Gymnasium.

The structure is a two-story steel truss covered in translucent white insulated panels. The panels at eye-level may be opened outward forming awnings over their sills. At night the interior lighting produces a glowing effect, lighting the axis and pathway below the bridge.

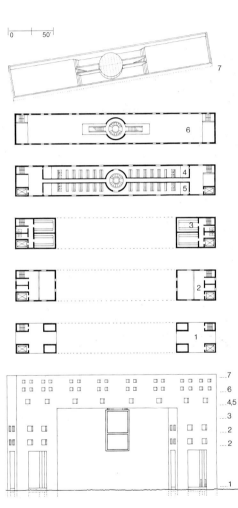

```
0        50'
```

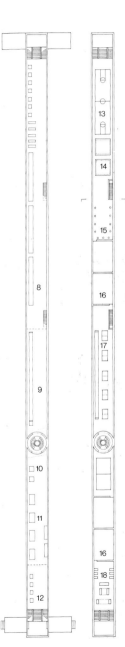

1. Docks.
2. Rowing club.
3. Steam rooms.
4. Men's lockers.
5. Women's lockers.
6. Ice skating rink.
7. Observcation deck.
8. Full shuffle board.
9. Walking belts.
10. Tournament arm wrestling.
11. Billiards.
12. Professional checkers.
13. "Long" basketball.
14. Boxing rings.
15. Boxing: light and heavy bags.
16. Handball courts.
17. Runing belts.
18. Weight training.

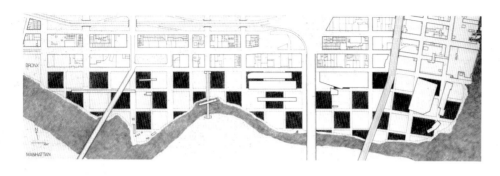

TELESCOPE HOUSE Still Pond, Maryland 1978.

With this project we launched our debate against eclecticism and against the importation of history. Eclecticism provokes the fragmentation of the past and the obfuscation of the present. This project is for us its opposite; it is a kind of distilled modern interpretation of certain cultural developments.

—Excerpt from exhibition, Yale University 1979

A retired couple with a very narrow site on Chesapeake Bay required a house in portions that could be closed off when not in use. This coincided with certain configurations observed in the history of Eastern Shore architecture. We fused a model of a particular type, the telescope house, with the program. Telescope houses, evolving since the early 1700s, received their name from their external appearance resembling a spyglass or telescope. Some were built large section first, descending, some small section first,

ascending, and some, all sections at once.

The proposed house is in three portions corresponding to frequency of use: a) the basic house for two persons, used year round; b) the formal entertainment rooms for visiting family; and c) the guest rooms, closed off when not in use.

The plan responds to a thin lot (160 feet by 493 feet) which is narrowed further by a 60 foot setback from the water edge and from the street. The house is approached from a long driveway framed with trees, which offers a glimpse of the bay before passing parallel to the house and court. Walking through the court onto the screened front porch, a grid of steel windows with double doors leads to the entrance hall and sitting room beyond. Moving through the house gives a feeling of crossing strips of sunlight aligned with views of the water, as each major room has both north and south windows of

identical exposure. The second level observatory can be reached by an interior stair or by way of the roof that ascends parallel to the water's edge. Magnificent vantage points facing the bay and the wild life preserve on the adjacent site can be found along the roof, in the observatory, and along the deck overlooking the courtyard. The house does not so much fill the site as create a new, synthetic one, looking over the trees to the Chesapeake.

The structure is of stained concrete block with wooden roof and floor joists. The rubber-membrane roof is of the type developed for commercial construction, eliminating the need for any roof flashing. Windows are painted steel with insulated glass. The cerulean blue concrete pavers of the entrance court lead to an entrance hall of honed marble slabs, which gives way to an assymetrical black slate stair leading to the observatory.

a. b. c.

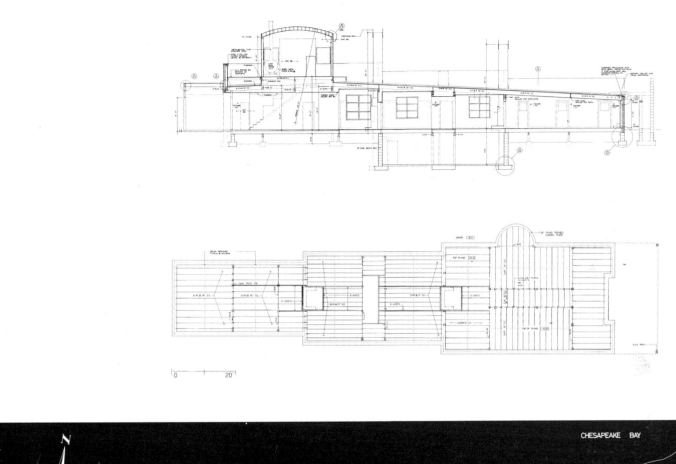

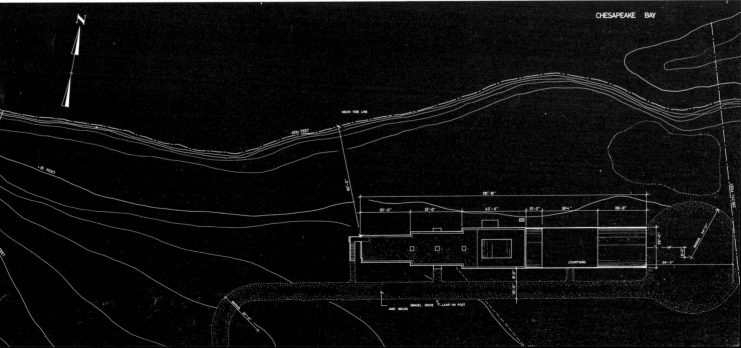

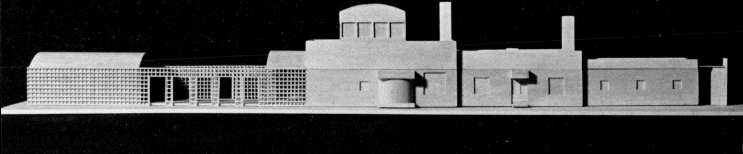

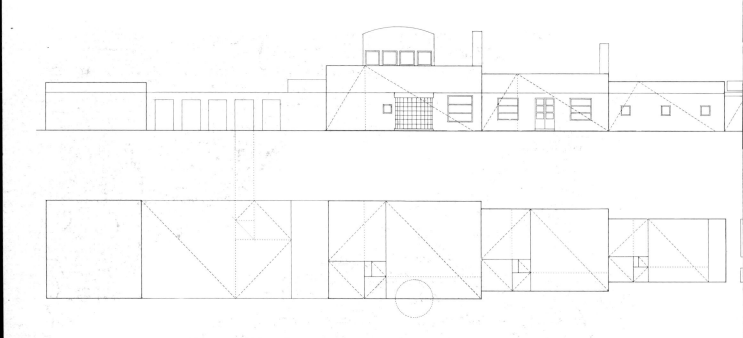

Proportion study.

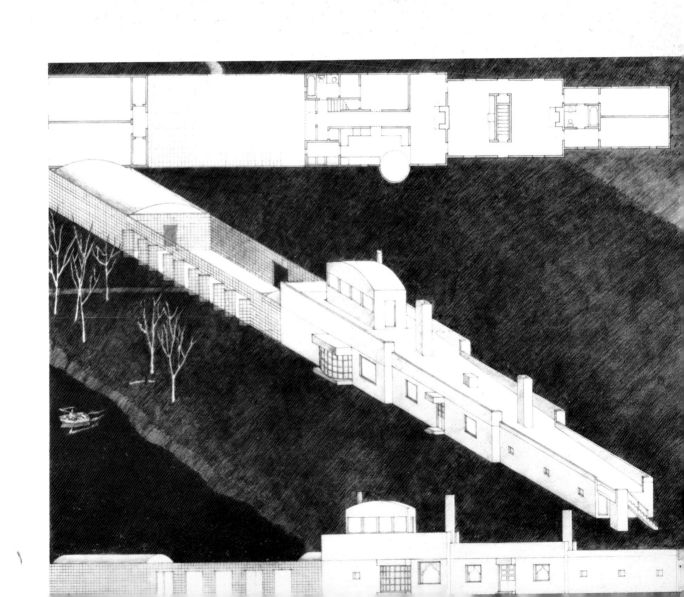

**COURTYARD ADDITION Millville, New Jersey
1978.** The client, an advertising agency specializing in small aircraft, has been using the existing nineteenth-century house for several years. The addition of five graphic arts work tables in a new workroom at the rear of the house suggested organizing the sunny side of the lot into a courtyard. This solution appealed in particular to the employees who feared that the addition would destroy existing grapevines that serve as an arbor for lunch in the summer.

The artists' work tables are aligned in the left wing with a window over each. The hollow right wing forms an entrance pavilion and provides space for further expansion. The recognition of the courtyard as the focus of the project exploited the minimum budget that precluded "embellishment" of the actual construction.

Formalization of vestigial space and irregular buildings into a rigorously composed court simultaneously reinforces the urban structure and protects and exalts the existing greenery. This suggests the role of architecture to propose a microcosmic urban unit that both intensifies and respects the form of this small town.

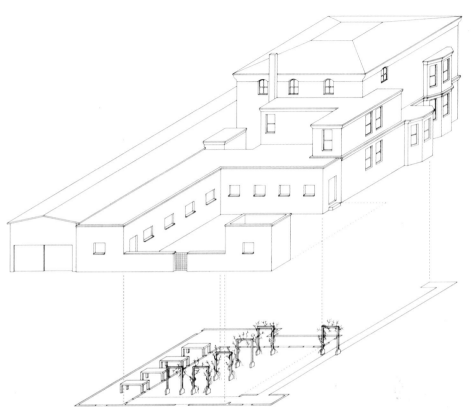

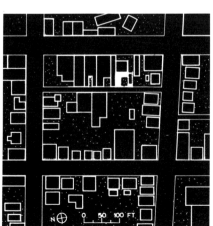

View of the courtyard addition in July, 1980. Two years after completion, the street-defining garden wall was imitated by the neighbor on the adjacent lot. No words were exchanged; he simply copied the example.

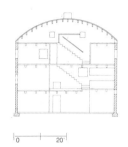

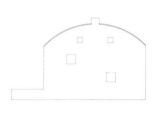

MINIMUM HOUSING Hastings-on-Hudson, New York 1977-8. Proposed for a site near Manhattan, the houses each have a little garden and a back porch. A collective green space is formed as a grass-covered, lozenge-shaped mound over a collectively-owned room.

As an alternative to high-rise housing with its isolation of the elderly, dangerous play areas for children, and so on, these houses have areas for playing, raising small animals, and for the elderly to rest on porches to view activities such as gardening. Construction of the 1300 square foot houses is in single span wood joists, concrete block walls, and rubber-membrane roofing and wall covering.

LES HALLES COMPETITION Paris, France 1979.

One main intention organizes this scheme: a compressed account of the site's history gives form to the grand urban place. Marble slabs mark the rectangles where the Les Halles pavilions of Baltard once stood. Trees are planted in place of the iron columns. The white marble slabs are inlaid with stone patterns demarking streets and buildings displaced by consecutive development on this ancient site.

The new place, of a volume on the order of Palais Royale, Place des Voges, and the Place du Carousel, has no aristocratic program of palatial residences to form its boundaries. Here instead is a chance for a twentieth-century place. The walls that bound it are lined with arcades made entirely of sandblasted glass. These translucent walls echo the events of this site since the destruction of the

stone "fortress" of 1853 and the subsequent creation of a new architecture of glass.

Houses of traditional color, with their backs to the arcade, face the city outside. The wall of housing is made up of two alternating building types, individually and vertically accessible, typical of the houses in this quarter. Each building contains approximately ten large apartments and has its own character of fenestration, roof, and color.

Sitting on the opposite end of a new axis to Centre Pompidou, our proposal is for an international place. Bustling with activity from the subterranean complex and the Plateau Beauborg, this vast opening is, at certain times, a place of crystalline silence. At night, with the frosted arcades and underground forum glowing, the splendor of a great capitol can be fully felt. The site has a memory of its own.

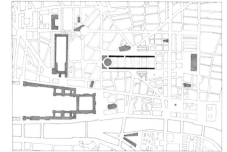

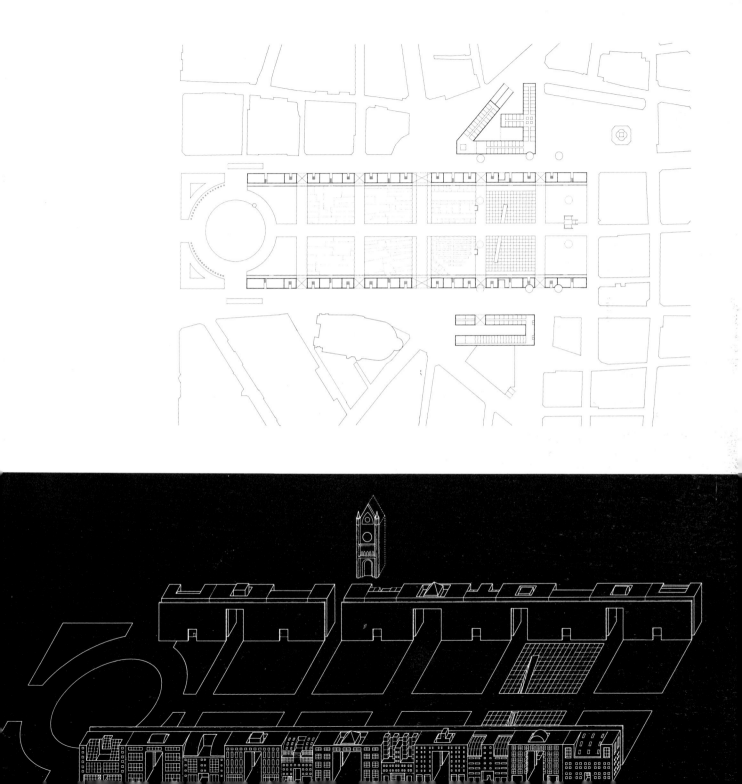

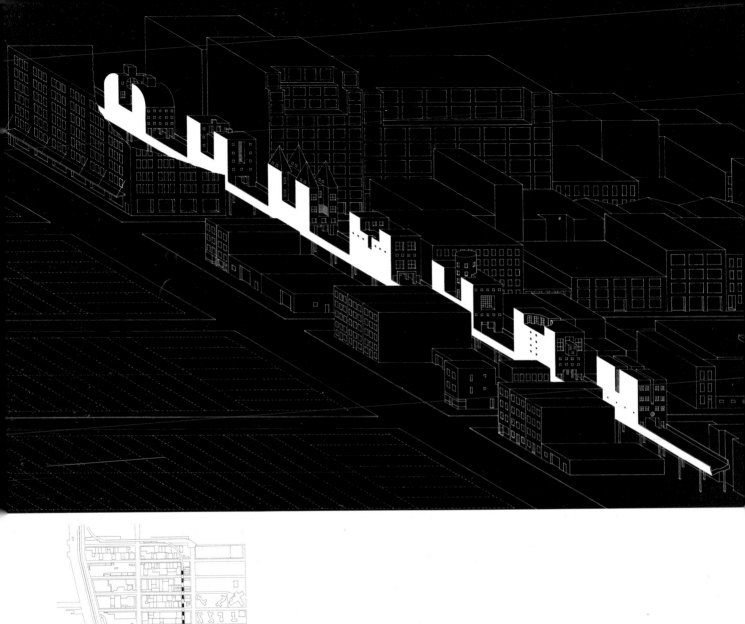

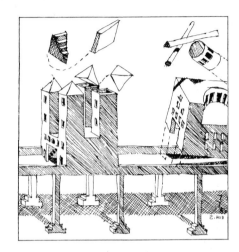

BRIDGE OF HOUSES New York, New York 1981.
The site and structural foundation of the Bridge of Houses is the existing superstructure of an abandoned elevated rail link in the Chelsea area of New York City. This steel structure is utilized in its straight leg from West 19th Street to West 29th Street parallel to the Hudson River.

West Chelsea is changing from a warehouse district to a residential area. With the decline of shipping activity on the pierfront, many vacant warehouses are being converted to residential lofts. The Bridge of Houses reflects the new character of the area as a place of habitation. Re-use rather than demolition of the existing bridge would be a per-

manent contribution to the character of the city.

This project offers a variety of housing types for the Chelsea area, as well as an elevated public promenade connecting with the new Convention Center on its north end. The structural capacity and width of the existing bridge determine the height and width of the houses. Four houses have been developed in detail, emphasizing the intention to provide a collection of housing blocks offering the widest possible range of social-economic coexistence. At one extreme are houses of single room occupancy type, offered for the city's homeless. Each of these blocks contains twenty studio rooms. At the other extreme are houses of luxury apartments; each of

these blocks contains three or four flats. Shops line the public promenade level below the houses.

The new houses are built in an alternating pattern with a series of 2,000 square foot courtyards (50% open space). All new houses align with the existing block front at the street walls, reinforcing the street pattern. The ornamental portions of the rail bridge that pass over the streets remain open.

Construction consists of a lightweight metal frame with a reinforced exterior rendering on wire lath and a painted finish. Windows have a baked enamel finish, while doors are made of solid core wood with sandblasted glass drawings on the entrances and brass lever handles.

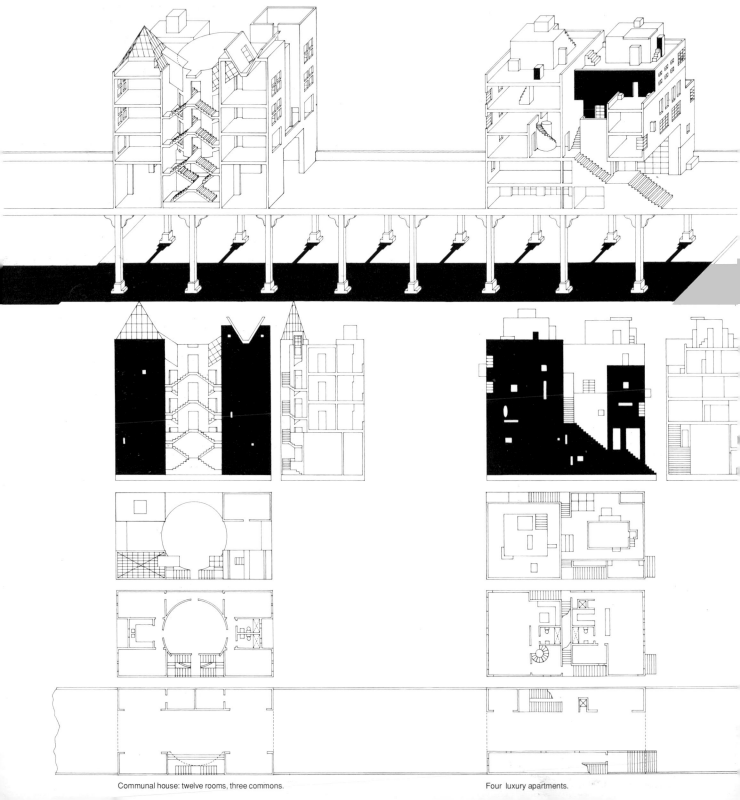

Communal house: twelve rooms, three commons.   Four luxury apartments.

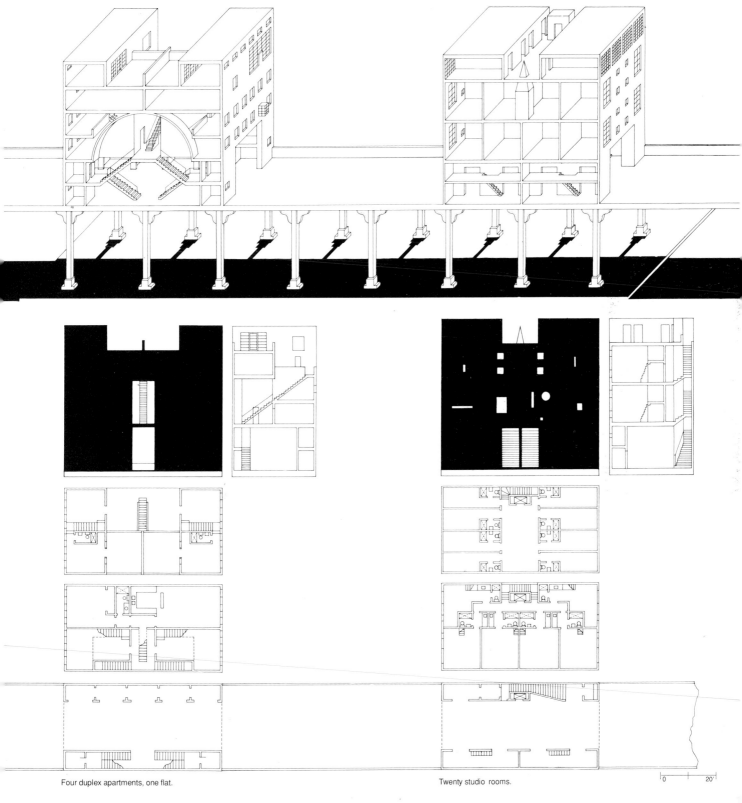

Four duplex apartments, one flat.   Twenty studio rooms.   0   20'

Left: Looking west on 20th Street.
Above: Exisiting abandoned bridge: a form leaving one
function behind to support another.

Above: The public promenade: a bridge is more than getting from one place to another; it is a statement of coexistence and diversity.
Overleaf: Bridge of Houses project (1979).

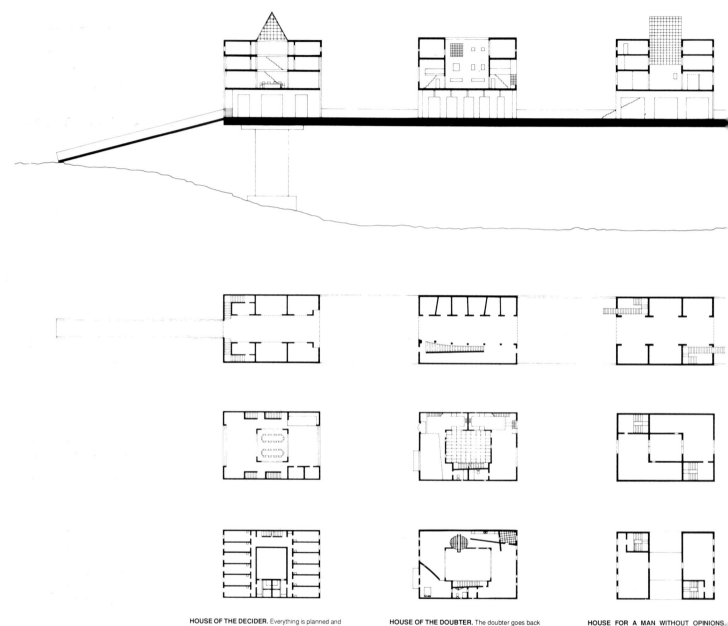

HOUSE OF THE DECIDER. Everything is planned and worked out; there are 24 sleeping rooms with a sink in every room. At the dining tables, on the floor of the courtyard there are 22 seats. Each day three people work in the kitchen. Each day one seat is reserved for a guest. Every morning breakfast is served at 6 a.m. Everyone gets an apple and a buckwheat pancake. Every menu has been planned in advance for three meals a day for the entire year. The annual menu varies for odd and even years. It is possible to predict exactly what will be served on a given day forty years into the future. There are no surprises in the House of the Decider.

HOUSE OF THE DOUBTER. The doubter goes back on everything he says . . . he never intends anything. If he makes a decision, it is by accident. Each morning when the doubter finally gets up (he is never satisfied with sleep), he dresses with great effort. When making decisions on what to wear, his mind wanders to scenes of humiliation in front of large assemblies. The doubter's meals are tenuous. In the process of indecision, he eats directly from the refrigerator shelf, randomly.

He listens to many voices each day, but is suspicious of them. He is most skeptical when hearing himself speak: the doubter makes statements that he cannot believe.

HOUSE FOR A MAN WITHOUT OPINIONS. house for the man without opinions is a series of rooms connected by a large central atrium filled birds. The birds fly around in the atrium all day while man with no opinions looks at them from every Several cats roam at random up and down the sta the house, pausing for naps on the landings. The ings are very large and the sight of the cats nappi them makes the man without opinions smile. How he has been told that the cats are tricky and opi ated, so he focuses on the birds.

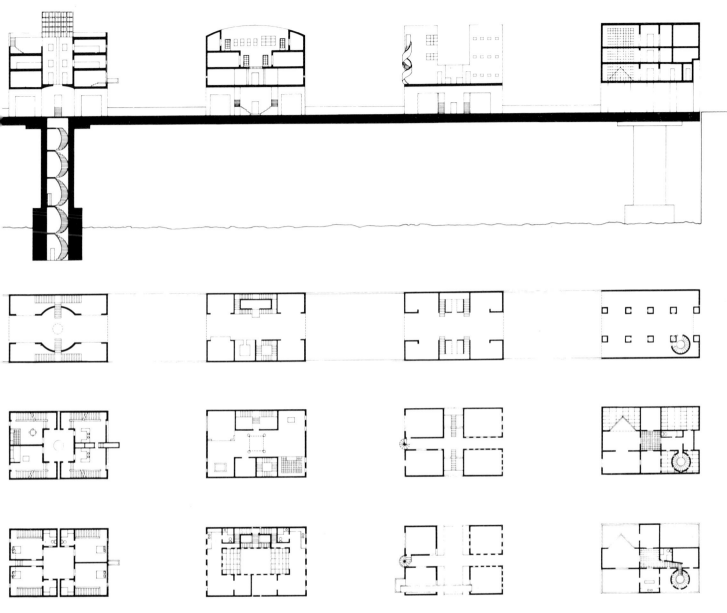

MIDDLE. This house, unlike the others on the [bridge] is completely divided crosswise by a slot, [leavi]ng a narrow slice of the view beyond. These [?] openings align with the rising sun on one side [and th]e setting sun on the other. Most days the mist [i]n the valley is so dense that the bridge seems [s]panning a clouded hollow. On clear days, there [is a gli]mpse of an ascending and descending land[scape i]n the distance.

[This] narrow view from the bridge is seldom seen by [those] who only pass for a visit; they are harassed by [do]gs who guard the ends of the bridge, barking [especi]ally with the occupation of any visitor. Only [those] who live on the bridge remain in neither "this [world n]or "other worlds."

DREAM HOUSE. The house is shaped like an upside-down dish, patterned from the vault of the sky. Carved from the center is a courtyard stepping down like a little canyon, a shallow pool of water at the floor. The inhabitants look into the pool but cannot see the bottom. No rays of sun reach the little pool, nor are beams of moonlight reflected. The lush green acanthus trees growing on the edges of the court do not appear on the mirror of water. No ripple breaks its surface, which ever reflects a void of absolutely dark night. In the silence of the courtyard, the inhabitants can hear (but cannot see) a steady dripping. Drop by drop this sound sets them dreaming.

FOUR TOWER HOUSE. The house is divided into four towers: the tower of work (to work is considered a privilege); the tower of sleep (a lunar tower of private chambers); the tower of recreation and friendship (which contains dining, lounging parlors, and exercising pools); and a tower of culture. From the tower of work, a diagonal ramp passes down through the tower of recreation and friendship. A thin, fragile stair spirals up from the floor of the courtyard to the tower of culture.

MATTER AND MEMORY. This house is on an end of the bridge (neither abutment is expressed as end or beginning). Matter, the activities of conscious day-to-day life, is formed into a cruciform describing four small outer courts. Within the cruciform are the living, dining, sleeping, and service areas. The four little courtyards, like the ante-chambers of the mind, are places of memory and contemplation.

43

METZ HOUSE Staten Island, New York 1980.
The site for this project is a thickly wooded lot on
Staten Island overlooking a forested ravine. It is an
inexpensive house for a young couple, both artists.
Conventional living and dining rooms are excluded
in favor of two larger studios and a large kitchen.
The studio's requirements reflect the nearly opposite sensibilities of the two artists: husband
(sculptor) and wife (painter). She makes floral
paintings, loves sunlight and plants, and has several cats. He makes black concrete sculpture, hates
cats and house plants, and doesn't care to have
natural light in his studio as he works mostly at
night. One bedroom is for a teenage daughter who
desires privacy. The client expressed dislike of the
suburban image of local developments, favoring

an approach that leaves all natural vegetation on
the site untouched.

The house is a dialectic of two parts based on
a traditional "U"-type courtyard plan. An introspec-
tive outdoor court opens to the sun and a view of
the ravine. The analogy of an urban building type,
like an island in the forest, is carried out in all the
elevations: the front facade is articulated in integral
color concrete blocks, the side walls are painted
black like the party walls in a city, and the courtyard
is painted white for maximum light.

Each wing of the "U" contains one of the
studios, whose character is expressed by the contrast between the two wings. In the right wing is the
painting studio with skylight providing indirect light.
Above the monitors is a ramp to the solitude of the

study. In the lower part of the left wing is the sculpture studio, opening to the grotto and outdoor work
area. The grotto receives light from cylindrical
glass block elements cast in the slab of the courtyard. In the center of the main level are the common areas of the kitchen/dining and entrance
foyer. The teenager's bedroom has a special roof,
giving her the feeling of being in a separate little
house.

Construction is insulation-filled concrete block
with plaster interiors applied directly to the block.
Floors are industrial grade pine with an oiled finish.
The roof is insulated wood framing with composite
roll-roofing. Interior stairs in the entrance foyer are
black slate alternating with white marble, creating
an effect like the black and white keys of a piano.

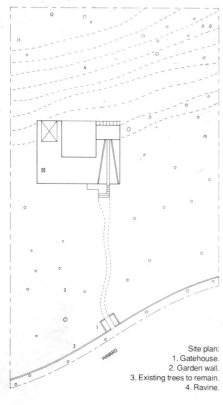

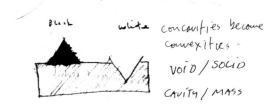

Black   white   concavities become
                  convexities -
                  VOID / SOLID
                  CAVITY / MASS

Site plan:
1. Gatehouse.
2. Garden wall.
3. Existing trees to remain.
4. Ravine.

HAWARD

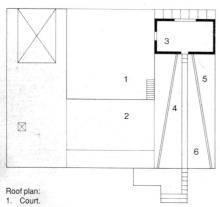

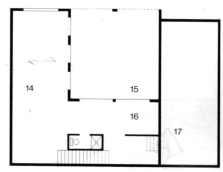

Roof plan:
1. Court.
2. Roof vegetable garden.
3. Study/Observatory.
4. Ramp to study.
5. Skylight monitors.
6. Solar plate.

Entry level:
7. Entry foyer.
8. Kitchen/Dining.
9. Bedroom.
10. Washer/Dryer.
11. Child's room.
12. Courtyard.
13. Upper studio (painting).

Lower level:
14. Lower studio (sculpture).
15. Grotto work area.
16. Utility.
17. Thermal storage.

0   10'

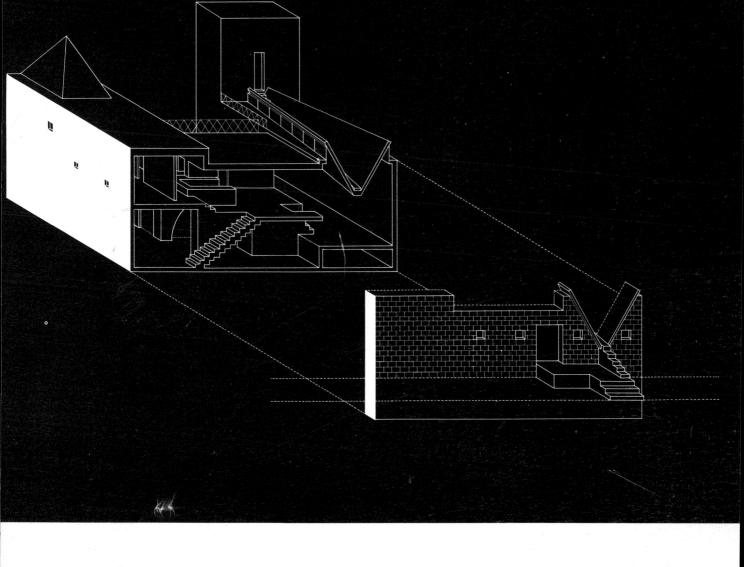

47

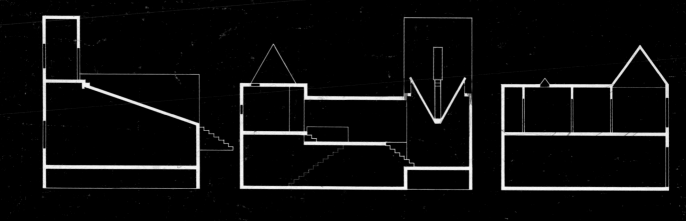

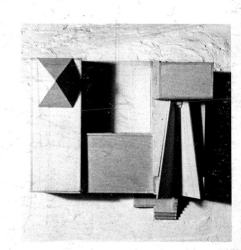

Left: Sections.
Below: Courtyard and exterior elevations.

Existing stone wall.

50

POOL HOUSE AND SCULPTURE STUDIO

Scarsdale, New York 1981. A sculpture studio and a bathhouse are sited next to an existing swimming pool. The bathhouse provides both a changing and refreshment area near the pool. The sculpture studio is situated adjacent to the bath house to enable it to function occasionally as a guest room.

The site in Scarsdale, New York has a history that dates from the transference of property rights by King George in the early eighteenth century. The land is marked by stone walls that were used to define its boundaries.

The project is organized with the idea of *walls within walls*. New walls enclosing the existing pool form a courtyard recalling the ancient stone boundary wall around the site. On the north wall of the new court, the pool house and sculpture studio form a two-story pavilion. The sculpture studio on the upper level receives light from two major windows and a pyramid skylight, which also marks the major axes on the site.

Construction is of insulation-filled concrete block with smooth plaster interiors and luminous grey stucco exteriors. Red integral color concrete pavers in the courtyard provide contrast with the dark green marble of the details and countertops. The floor of the bathhouse is flesh-colored marble. The white ceramic tile of the shower room is broken by a green marble water column with brass shower fixtures. Glass openings in the lower doors have sandblasted drawings carved in them that relate to the history of the site and the architectonic ideas.

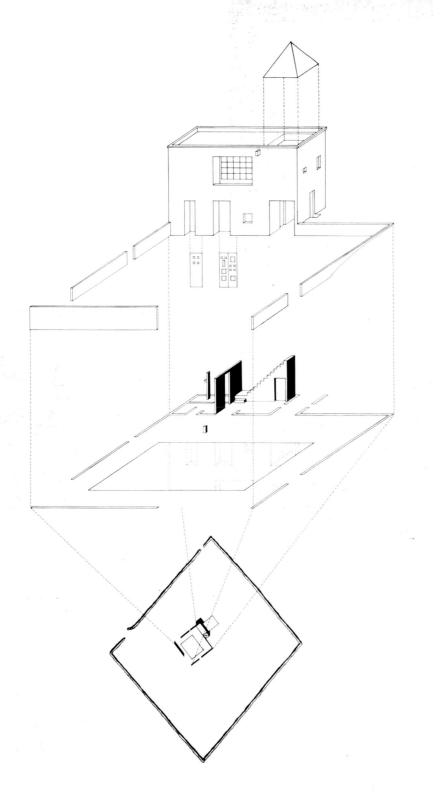

1. Passage.
2. Pool house.
3. Sculpture studio.

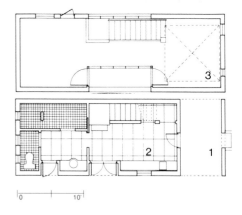

0   10'

52

Right: Sandblasted glass details.
Forms in top pane are transformed
by their "reflection" in the pool.

GUARDIAN SAFE DEPOSITORY Fair Lawn, New Jersey 1983. The renovation of an existing concrete block building into a safe depository bank included the construction of a new facade, a new lobby, new private offices, special security systems, and a large vault constructed of 1/2" thick steel plates.

The building plan is arranged from the most rational and dense at the rear (rows of steel safe deposit boxes) to the most irrational and thin at the front (public lobby). The public parts of the building—the front facade and lobby—are joined where the circle of the lobby intersects the facade in a gridded plane of glass, opening the space to public view. The remainder of the public side has steel

windows set into sky blue stucco on marble sills. Side walls are black stucco, emphasizing the facade while recalling party-wall building types in the old town of Fair Lawn.

Instead of the friezes or ornaments of a traditional public lobby, the visitor here encounters the record of an architectural inquiry comparing proportional order to musical harmony and ancient geometrical concepts. The seventeenth-century concept of "Harmony of the Spheres" together with the interpretations of proportion and harmony of the mathematician Johannes Kepler, inspired a planetary frieze circling the top of the lobby wall. Cubic interpretations of the nine planets are bent by the curvature of the space. Jupiter—the largest,

most prominent planet—is centered over the electronically controlled entrances to the vaults, its moons drifting along the lobby curve toward the rings of Saturn.

The proportions used throughout the structure are depicted directly in the logarithmic spiral forming the steel mullion divisions in the entry vestibule. Sandblasted glass drawings form a base to the vestibule recording all the concepts explored. Panels on the exterior faces of the vestibule depict separate concepts, while on the interior faces a concept's counterpoint is drawn. For example, Kepler's 1596 diagram comparing the five regular solids to the (then) six planets has a contemporary disordered counterpoint.

54

Left: Etched glass detail showing
dislocated Kepler's diagram.

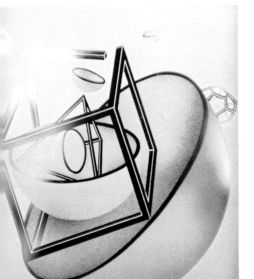

1. Entry vestibule.
2. Public lobby.
3. Access control.
4. Control doors.
5. Booths.
6. Vault.
7. Media vault.
8. Mechanical.
9. Conference rooms.
10. Offices.
11. Toilets.
12. Post office.
13. Private lobby.

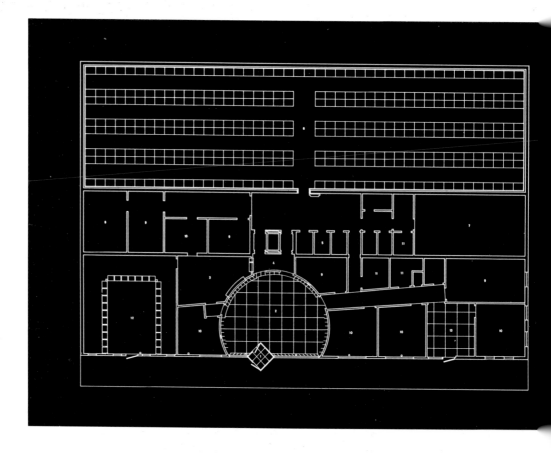

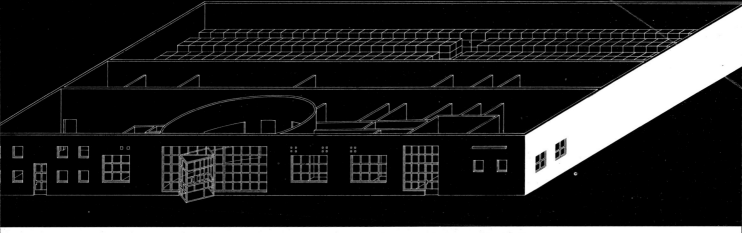

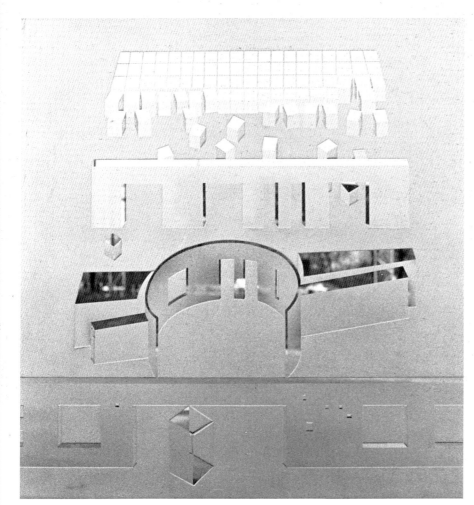

The luminous grey walls of the rotunda-like volume have a cream-colored terrazzo base with zinc strips in a stitching that runs counter to the rotation induced by the planetary frieze.

Note: The price of gold descended months after the building was completed, eroding the developer's purpose. The facility was demolished in 1985. Every glass drawing was destroyed.

VAN ZANDT HOUSE East Hampton, New York

1983. The two-acre site is in a heavily wooded area of large old trees near a potato field on the South Fork of Long Island. In this ancient forest, there is no context of provincial architecture. The only traces of man-made work are long mounds of earth (locally known as slave mounds), which thread through the trees leaving a broken record of early settlers' property lines.

The year-round weekend house includes a "lap pool" (an 18' x 60' swimming pool primarily used for exercise) and is intended to have "a sense of being with the trees." From the client's first letter: "It is important for me to have two separate elements to the house where I live, with my bedroom and bath and, at some opposite quarter, two guest rooms and a bath . . . ." Also requested was a screened porch, a large master bathroom with a steam shower, a dining area separate from the kitchen, and a living room with a stone fireplace.

The center and heart of the scheme is the void of the pool, reflecting the site's ancient trees and the sky; the two building elements, the main house and the guest house, frame this central place without making it an insistent focus. The double house concept aims at the creation of a place instead of a house/object.

The pool court runs east-west, but the houses' views are north-south. This arrangement results in many different views into the trees as well as maximum privacy for each bedroom. The main living room on the second level allows for the best views and breezes through north-south aligned windows as well as a roof form giving the room a special character. The kitchen is located between the winter dining room and a screened porch for summer dining at poolside. The end walls of the houses, aligned with the edge of the pool, are doubled in the water's reflection from either direction of approach, forming a little urban place like a slice of Venice in the forest.

In the history of American houses, the scheme is a two-story American "dog trot" type house, opened up with a pool inserted; in Germanic history, the houses recall the "fighting brothers" castles that face each other over the Rhine.

The construction is wood frame with integral color stucco rendering and terne metal roofing. Double glazed windows include large south facing window/doors at dining and entry that store sun-generated heat in the bluestone flooring. The dark integral color gunnite pool is heated by the sun.

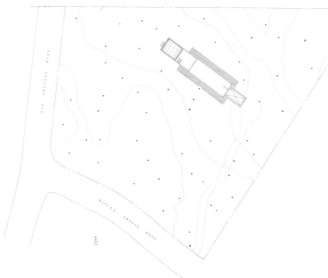

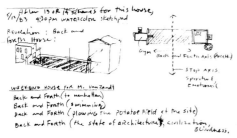

5/12/83 After 13 or 14 schemes for this house, 4:30 pm watercolor sketchpad

Revelation: Back and forth House!

Gym — Back and forth axis (arch.)

Stop axis
Spiritual
Emotional

WEEKEND HOUSE FOR Mr. VanZandt
Back and Forth (to Manhattan)
Back and Forth (swimming)
Back and Forth (plowing the potatoe field at the site)
Back and Forth (the state of architecture, civilization, blindness.

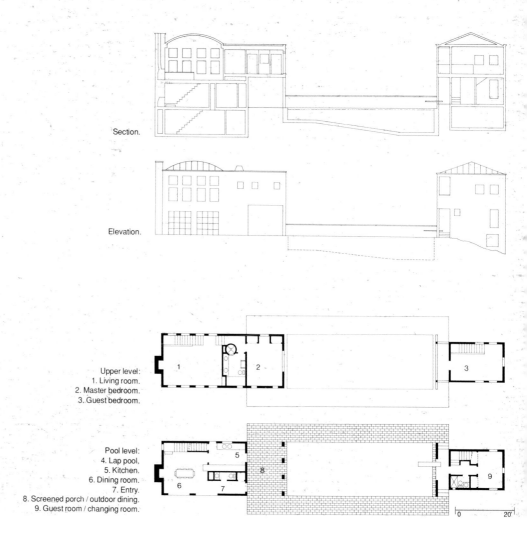

Section.

Elevation.

Upper level:
1. Living room.
2. Master bedroom.
3. Guest bedroom.

Pool level:
4. Lap pool.
5. Kitchen.
6. Dining room.
7. Entry.
8. Screened porch / outdoor dining.
9. Guest room / changing room.

0   20'

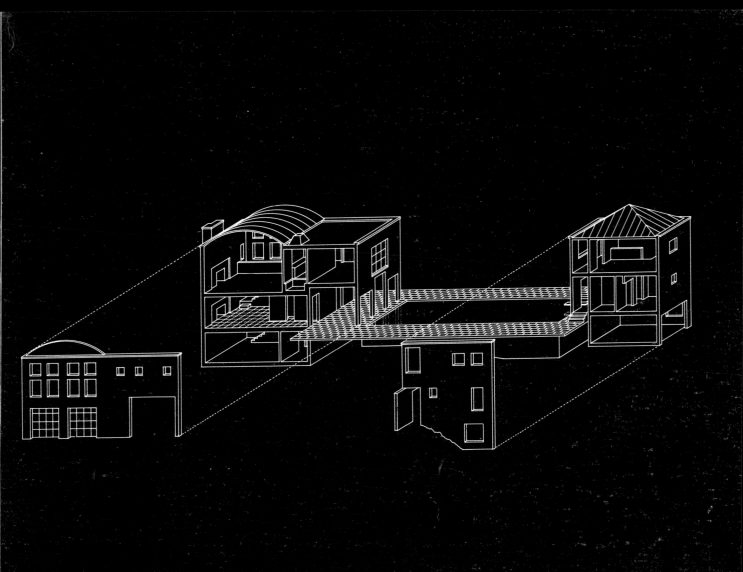

61

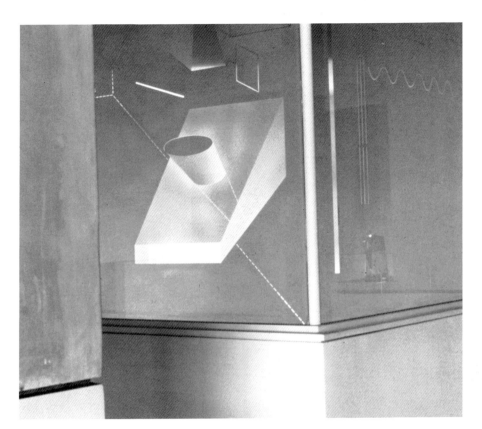

FIFTH AVENUE APARTMENT New York, New York 1983. The existing rooms were removed, exposing an uneven slab and beam system (1939) in the "L" shaped apartment. All views from the apartment are characterized by vertical buildings in the near distance.

A brass channel horizon line is set into the wall all around the "L." Above the channel (which is also a plaster screed), integral color blue plaster is applied to the random beam and plate configuration, resulting in an Euclidian cloud formation. The plaster sky with flying lamps hovers over a floor of waxed cork. Inside the "L" an investigation of elemental architectural composition is explored in three modes: the linear, the planar, and the volumetric.

The dining area is of a linear mode: a linear chandelier is made of three types of lines, a linear table with four linear chairs sits on a carpet patterned with a great variety of lines.

The living area is of a volumetric mode with stuffed cylindrical sofa cushions, a volumetric coffee table and a volumetric carpet.

The studio and bedroom are in a planar mode with a planar drawing board, planes of walls that unfold becoming doors, and a carpet with woven planar elements. An "L" shaped wall dividing the apartment from the entrance foyer records this investigation in a progression of sandblasted glass drawing: planar, volumetric, linear.

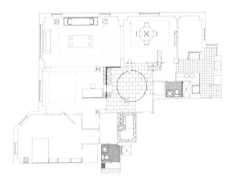

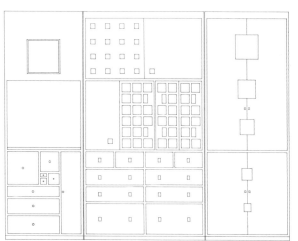

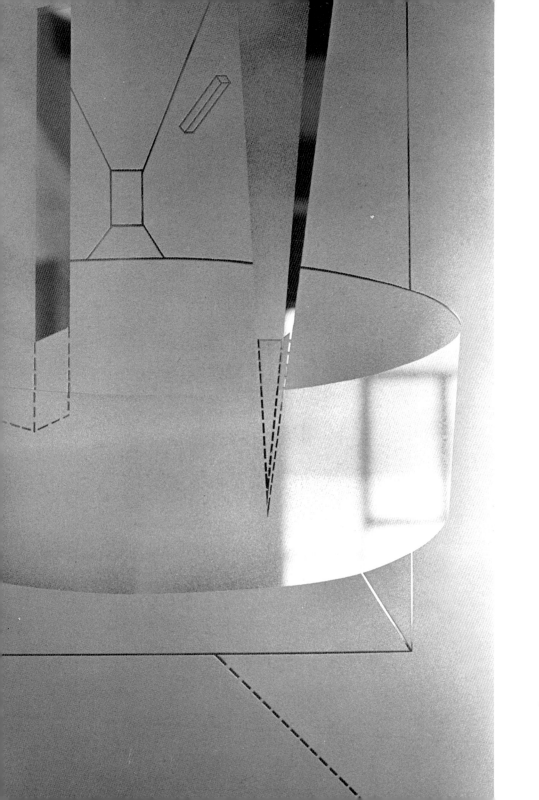

AUTONOMOUS ARTISANS' HOUSING Staten Island, New York 1980–84. An existing warehouse is converted to work space held in common by artisans working in several disciplines. Against the warehouse wall, houses are built in a pattern allowing for private gardens between each house. The plan/section is based on the shotgun type.

The individual autonomous artisan's craft is ex-pressed in the second level of each house: the paper maker's has a roof terrace shaped specifically for drying paper; the wood worker's house displays the skills of a boat builder; the mason has a brick barrel vault roof. A roof of etched glass covers the glass etcher's entry way. Similarly, expressions of craft exist in the plasterer's and metal worker's houses.

Outdoor areas include private gardens between each of the houses, as well as roof terraces. The urban street edge is maintained with the alignment of the front walls. Construction of the foundation level of each house is insulation-filled concrete block and wood floor joists. Roofs and second level elements are in different materials according to each artisan/occupant.

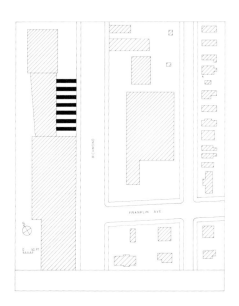

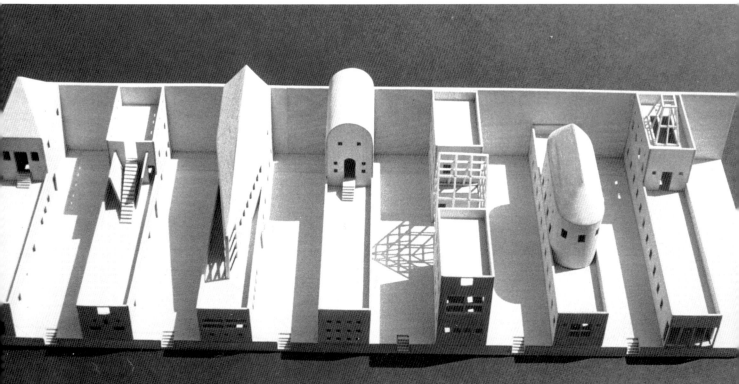

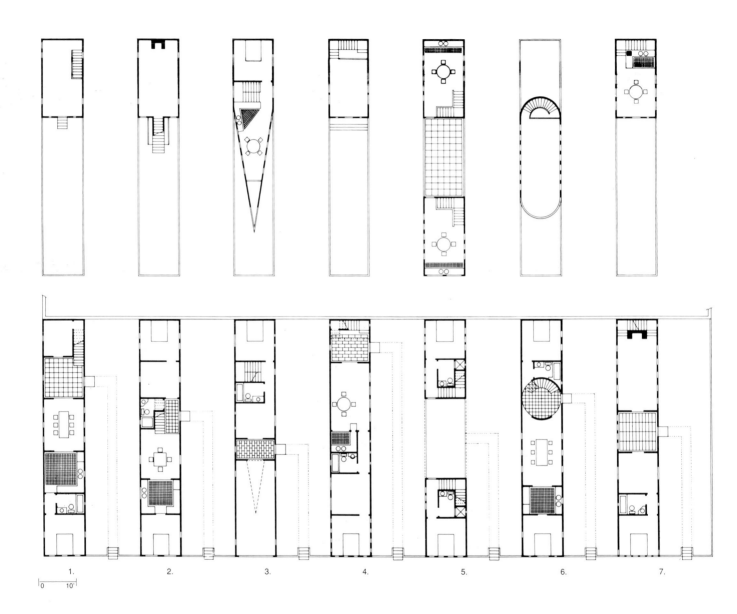

1.   2.   3.   4.   5.   6.   7.

0   10'

1. Tin bender's house.
2. Paper maker's house.
3. Wood worker's house.
4. Mason's house.
5. Glass etcher's house.
6. Plasterer's house.
7. Metal worker's house.

OCEANFRONT HOUSE Leucadia, California 1984. Situated on the top of a 97 foot bluff at the edge of the Pacific Ocean with the San Andreas Fault very near by, the site is fixed with a view across the infinite horizon of the Pacific.

It is a feeling of curious melancholy that dominates this view from its "edge of the world" site. In creating a setting for this, an almost Calvinistic silence is needed. Rather than a false positivism or an unwarranted negativism, we are trying for an unfolding condition—without hopefulness, without despair.

In response to the meditative site, the central portion of the house is a huge opening onto the oceanic horizon. The body of the house bridges this opening with a section of overlapping volumes topped by an arced roof. This bridge-over portion abuts a walled-out portion, making a clear distinction between Eastern and Western in the plan.

The planning codes of the California Coastal Commission provide an allowance of one foot of bluff erosion per year. This, together with a life span of 40 years, results in a strict 40' setback law from the top of the ocean bluff. The irregular bluff indention at the edge of the site determined the angle of the main body of this house relative to the street.

Grade level:
1. Entry foyer.
2. Dining room.
3. Kitchen.
4. Court.
10. Study.
11. Sauna, below.
12. Garage.

Upper level:
5. Living room.
6. Terrace.
7. Library.
8. Master bedroom.
9. Bedroom.

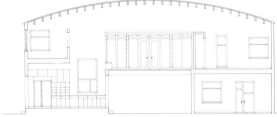

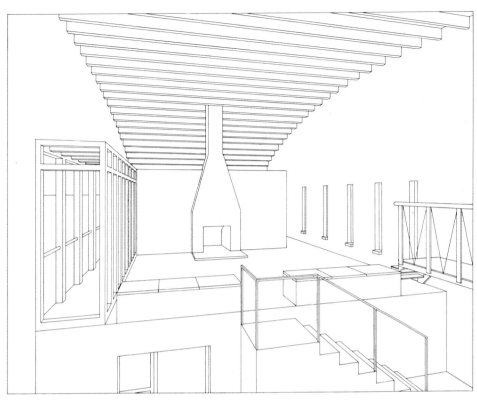

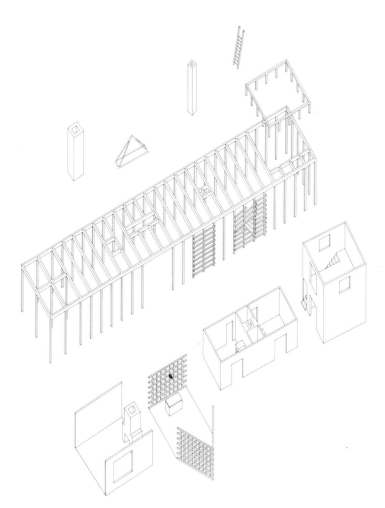

BERKOWITZ HOUSE Martha's Vineyard, Massachusetts 1984. "*In looking at things spiritual, we are too much like oysters observing the sun, through the water, and thinking that thick water the thinnest of air.*"—Herman Melville, *Moby Dick*

The site is a hill overlooking the Atlantic Ocean. The ground, densely overgrown with brush, is cut by a gully that descends to an unobstructed bog. The steep terrain and other building restrictions strictly limit the siting and construction material as well as the building height for the vacation home.

According to Melville's *Moby Dick*, the Indian tribe that originally inhabited Martha's Vineyard created a unique dwelling type. Finding a whale skeleton on the beach, they would pull it up to dry land and stretch skins or bark over it, transforming it into a house.

The house is an inside-out balloon frame of wooden construction; a skeleton house whose modern bones define a veranda. Along this continuous porch, wooden members receive the natural vines of the island, which transform the straight linear mode of the architecture.

The structural frame exposed inside and out meets the undisturbed sand dune on point foundations rather than on a common perimeter footing. Roofing is a rubber membrane unrolled over the frame, analogous to the skins over the whale skeleton.

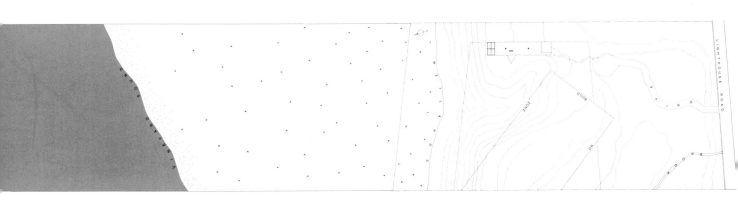

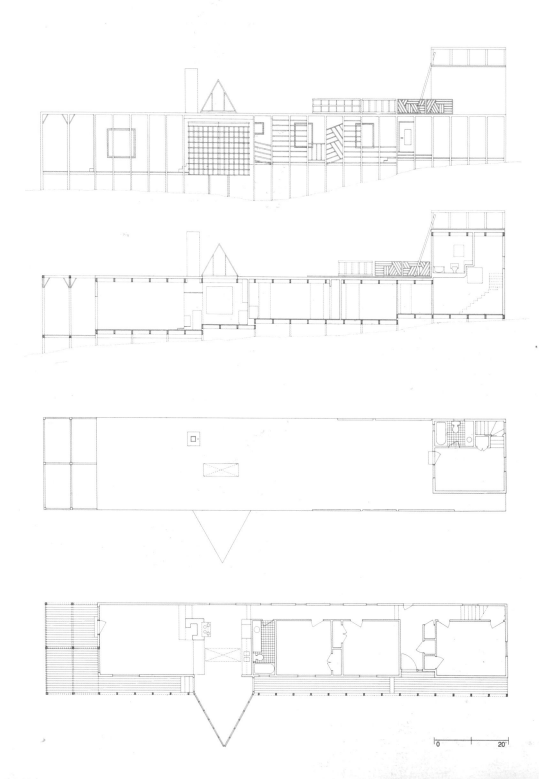

0   20'

Below: A skeleton of shadows moves across the veranda.

77

Point foundations.

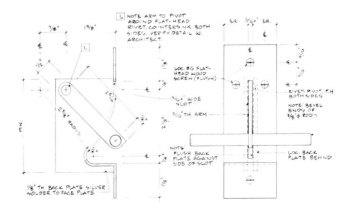

Detail of door pull.

Construction view from west.

Model from east.

HYBRID BUILDING Seaside, Florida 1985–88.

Seaside is a new town currently under construction on the Gulf of Mexico. The planners have established height restrictions, design guidelines, and easements. By their code, this project and adjoining buildings are required to form a continuous public arcade around a new public square.

The proposal is a Hybrid Building, combining retail, office, and residential uses. The concentration of disjointed programs forms an incidental urbanism. Along with the intensification of an urban condition, we propose a formation of a "society of strangers." The building forms split at the upper levels into East and West types. Those facing the setting sun and central square are rooms for boisterous types, late risers who enjoy watching the action, toasting the sunset, etc. All of their two-level flats are identical. They contain luxury bathrooms, microwave ovens, and space for parties.

Facing east to the morning sun are rooms for melancholic types. These individuals are early risers, inclined to silence and solitude. Melancholic types are imagined as a tragic poet, a musician, and a mathematician. The plans and sections of the three rear flats are characterized accordingly. The house of the tragic poet has dim light; every window is of the same narrow and tall dimension. The awning at the roof is like a rag on a peasant's table. In the house of the musician, light is cast down from corner windows on the upper level. A black plaster wall slips from the lower to the upper floor enhancing the flowing nature of the space. In the house of the mathematician, everything is slightly warped. The stair to the second level warps over the bathroom; the warp of the ceiling joists forms a slight double-curved surface. At the second level is a calculating table with a skull shelf, in homage to Johannes Kepler.

Construction is of precast concrete columns, beams, and hollow-core planks. Walls are integral color stucco on concrete block; roofs are galvanized metal.

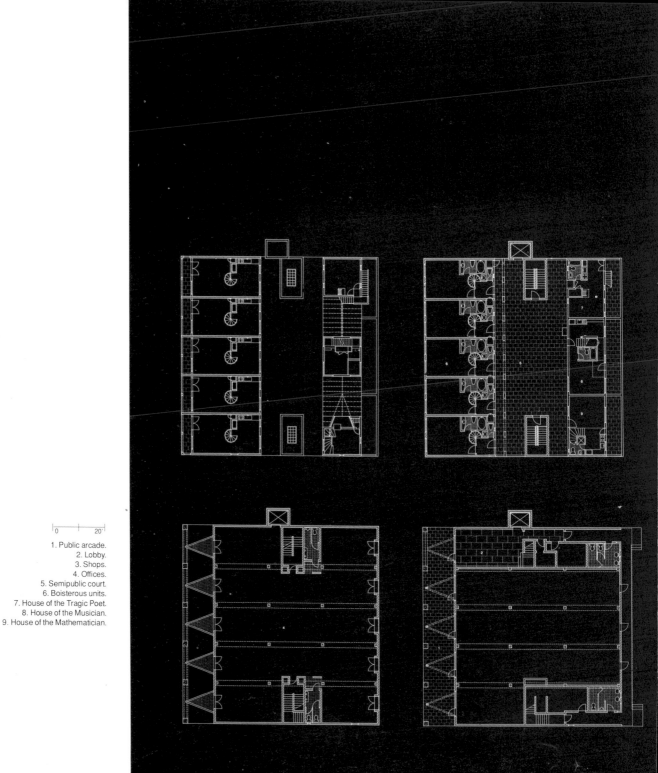

1. Public arcade.
2. Lobby.
3. Shops.
4. Offices.
5. Semipublic court.
6. Boisterous units.
7. House of the Tragic Poet.
8. House of the Musician.
9. House of the Mathematician.

0   20'

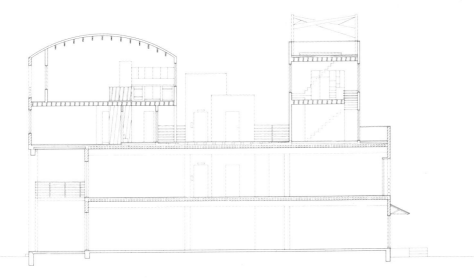

Precast beams, columns,
and planks before slab pour.

83

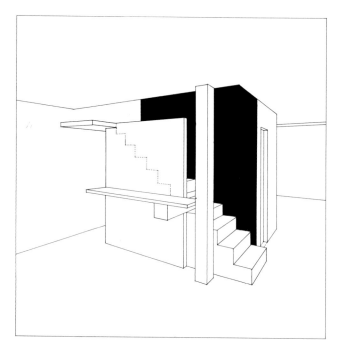

Right: House of the Musician.
Below: House of the Tragic Poet.

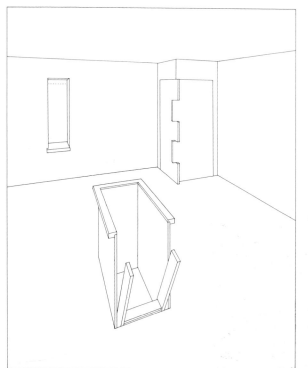

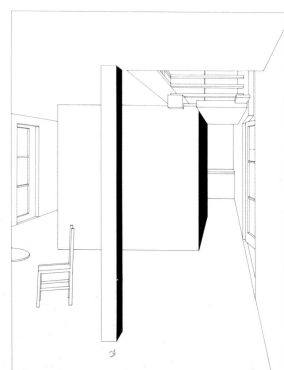

84

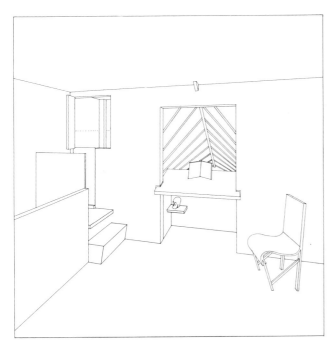

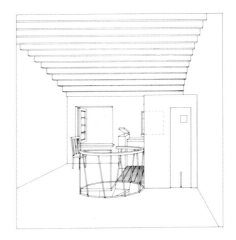

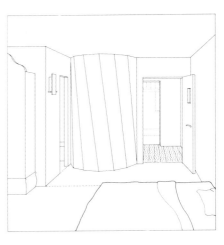

Above: Boisterous units.
Above left: House of the Mathematician.
Below: Under construction.

Perspective of east elevation.

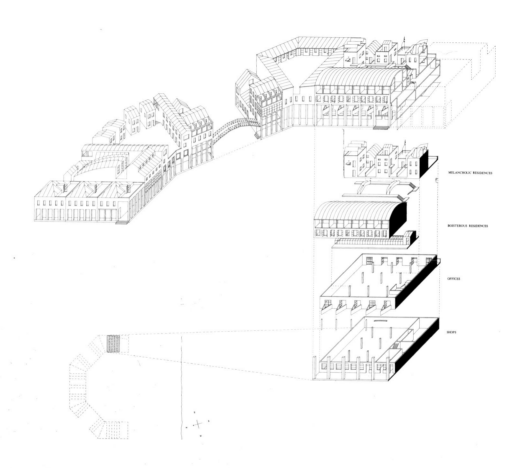

MELANCHOLIC RESIDENCES

BOISTEROUS RESIDENCES

OFFICES

SHOPS

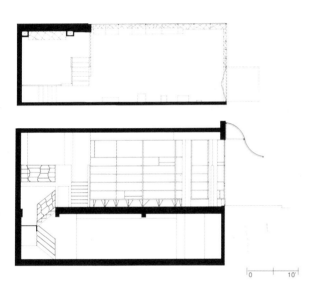

0   10'

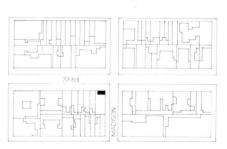

72 nd

MADISON

PACE SHOWROOM New York, New York 1986.
The site for the Pace Collection showroom is an existing two-story limestone structure with the corner of the building sliced back. A new foundation at the edge of the urban grid was set for the new showroom, completing the corner with a steel-mullioned window affording the maximum showroom glass.

An individual standing on a corner of a Manhattan intersection like Madison Avenue and 72nd Street is exposed to a hyperactive view of alternating forces of movement. The intersection is a counterpoint of one thing against another—fast against slow, stop against go—with the ominous command from the metropolitan authority, "Don't block the box."

An idea of counterpoint ("note against note") characterizes the essentially linear architecture. Small sandblasted amber glass panels are set against the horizontal steel bars of the main mullions. Along 72nd Street, the bars are predominantly horizontal, while along Madison they are predominantly vertical. The sandblasted glass drawings carry the contrapuntal idea to the detail scale. Along Madison Avenue, these drawings are in lines, while the 72nd Street facade shows the same drawings extruded into planes. It is as if the shop itself were a block of wood with end grain and edge grain differentiation. Each glass drawing freely interprets counterpoint in a different way, contrasting two kinds of lines, straight against curved, free form against arc, arc against zigzag, arc against chord, etc. The awning is a curve against the straight lines of the mullions. Inside, the idea is carried further in the guardrail where a curve fuses against simple horizontal bars dislocating them vertically to miss connecting along the curve. The ceiling is a free contrapuntal arrangement of rectangular voids (containing lighting and A.C.) set against the flat horizontal plane.

91

Arc against cord.

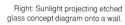
Right: Sunlight projecting etched glass concept diagram onto a wall.

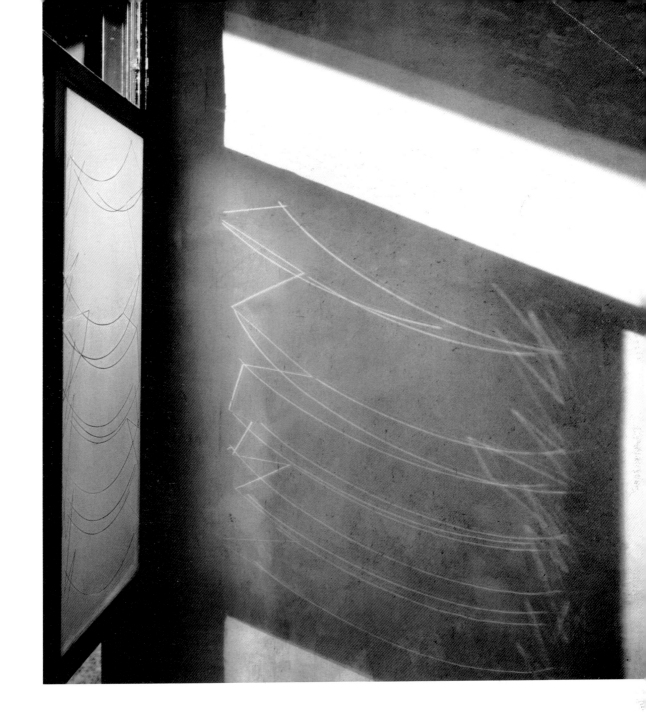

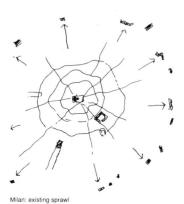

Milan: existing sprawl

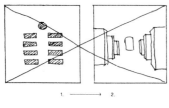

Dense outer ring contains the
city and clarifies the landscape.

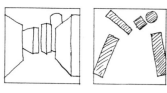

From perspective to space.

PORTA VITTORIA Milan, Italy 1986. The site for this project, commissioned by the XVII Triennale of Milan, is a disused freight rail yard, (part of Milan's old railroad belt), bordered by blocks of different housing types. It is in the nineteenth-century gridded portion of Milan, outside the historical center.

The program required keeping only the new "Passante" subway station, provoking the redevelopment of the area. Other functions to be located at the site include a bus station and garage for thirty buses, an air terminal station, hotels, offices, and housing. The proposal is also meant to provoke consideration of other programs for the reclamation of this metropolitan site.

The conviction behind this project is that an open work—an open future—is a source of human freedom. To investigate the uncertain, to bring out unexpected properties, to define psychological space, to allow the modern soul to emerge, to propose built configurations in the face of (and fully accepting) major social and programmatic uncertainty: this is our intention for the continuation of a "theoretical Milan."

From a dense center, Milan unfolds in circles ringed by a patchwork grid that finally sprawls raggedly into the landscape. Against this centrifugal urban sprawl (from dense core to light periphery), a reversal is proposed: light and fine-grained toward the center, heavy and volumetric toward the periphery. This proposal projects a new ring of density and intensity, adjoining the rolling green of a reconstituted landscape.

Three traditional urban strategies were rejected. The flexible planning device of the grid was suspended, because of its tendency to render everything as a measure of block-by-block infill. Secondly, the method that organizes historically modeled building types according to the existing morphology of the city was suspended. Finally, the whole method of drawing a plan layout, followed later by a three-dimensional form, was rejected.

The strategy used reverses the usual method of design in architecture (from plan to section, elevation, perspectival space). Instead, perspective sketches of spatial conditions are cast backward into plan fragments, which are then reconciled in an overall layout.

By its nature the perspective drawing implies associations between elements. These spatial configurations are taken as evidence of a particular activity, clues for reconstructing a program. Images of human activity, collected from diverse sources, are held alongside the perspective views to provoke the analysis.

Milan's Canals:
past and present.

97

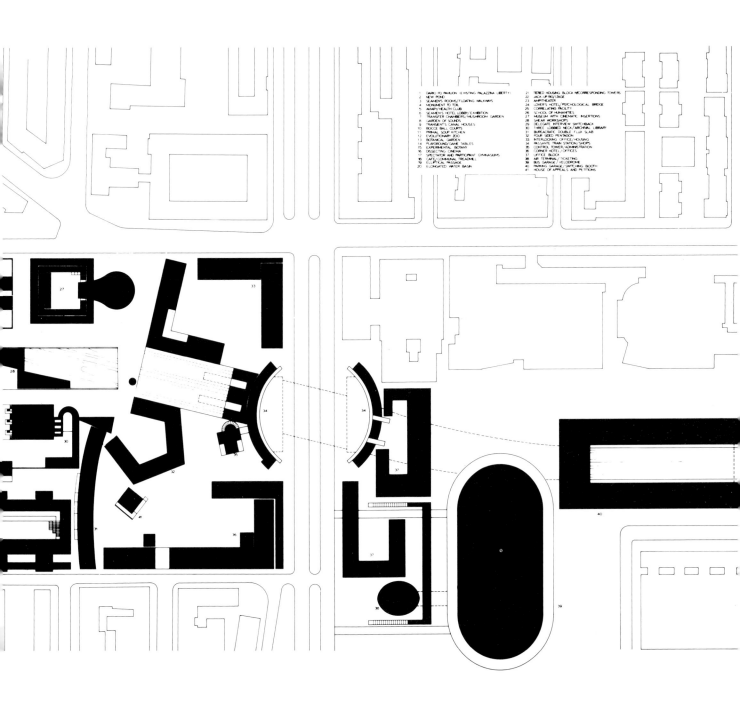

1   DARIO FO PAVILION (EXISTING PALAZZINA LIBERTY)
2   NEW POND
3   SEAMEN'S ROOMS/FLOATING WALKWAYS
4   MONUMENT TO TOIL
5   AVIARY/HEALTH CLUB
6   SEAMEN'S HOTEL LOBBY/EXHIBITION
7   TRANSFER CHAMBERS/MUSHROOM GARDEN
8   GARDEN OF SOUNDS
9   TRANSIENT'S CANAL HOUSES
10 BOCCE BALL COURTS
11 PRIMAL SOUP KITCHEN
12 EVOLUTIONARY ZOO
13 BOTANICAL GARDEN
14 PLAYGROUND/GAME TABLES
15 EXPERIMENTAL BOTANY
16 DISSECTING CINEMA
17 SPECTATOR AND PARTICIPANT GYMNASIUMS
18 CAFE/COMMUNAL TREADMILL
19 ELLIPTICAL PASSAGE
20 ELONGATED WATER BASIN

21 TIERED HOUSING BLOCK W/CORRESPONDING TOWERS
22 JACK-UP RIG/STAGE
23 AMPHITEATER
24 LOVER'S HOTEL/PSYCHOLOGICAL BRIDGE
25 CORRELATING FACILITY
26 SCHOOL OF HUMANITIES
27 MUSEUM WITH CINEMATIC INSERTIONS
28 SHEAR WORKSHOPS
29 DELEGATE INTERVIEW SWITCHBACK
30 THREE LOBBIED NEON/ARCHIVAL LIBRARY
31 BUREAUCRATIC DOUBLE FLUR SLAB
32 FOUR SIDED PENTAGON
33 INTERLOCKING OFFICE/HOUSING
34 PASSANTE TRAIN STATION/SHOPS
35 CONTROL TOWER/ADMINISTRATION
36 CORNER HOTEL/OFFICES
37 OFFICE BLOCK
38 AIR TERMINAL/TICKETING
39 BUS GARAGE/VELODROME
40 PARKING GARAGE/SWITCHING BOOTH
41 HOUSE OF APPEALS AND PETITIONS

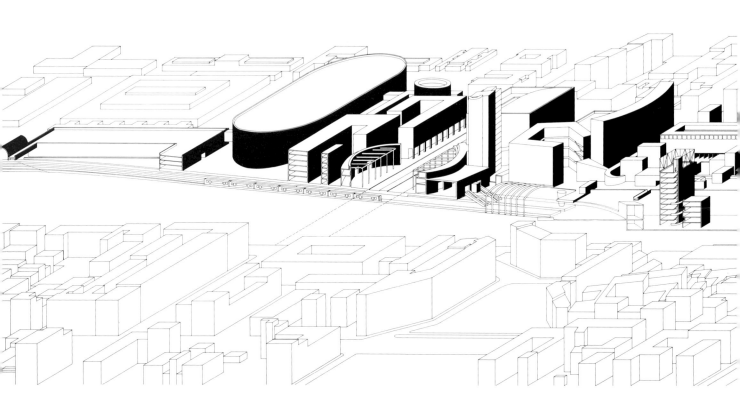

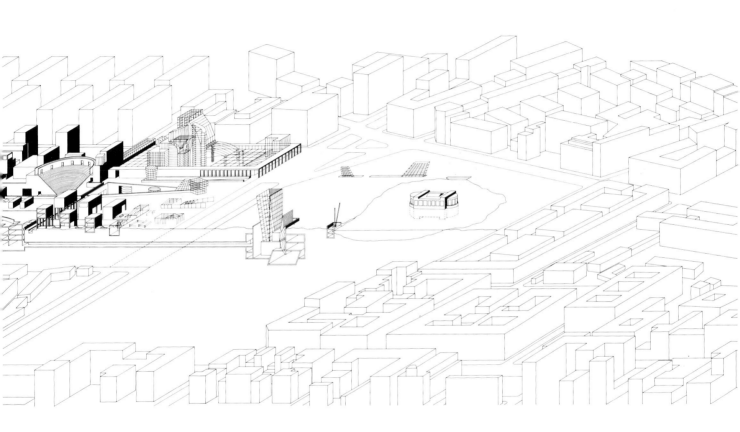

101

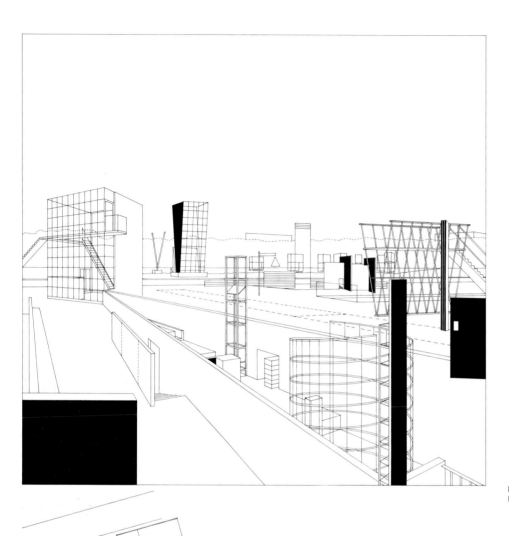

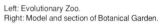

Left: Evolutionary Zoo.
Right: Model and section of Botanical Garden.

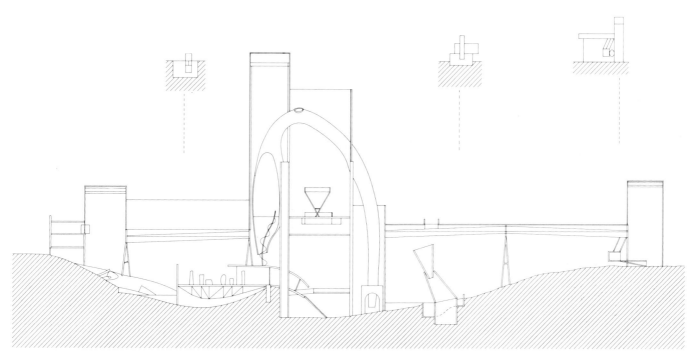

Botanical Garden section.

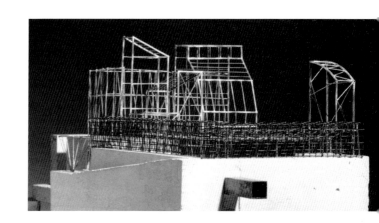

For the existing park, Largo Marinai d'Italia, a giant pond is proposed to reconcile the park with its name. The Palazzine Liberty is restored as the Dario Fo Pavilion and is accessible by rowboat only. A series of floating walkways connects a seaman's exhibition: residential apartments hover over tiny objects: an oar, a horn, a carving. Old sailors discuss the artifacts with passing visitors; stories are the material of the floating exhibition.

At the edge of the pond is a large metronome-like Monument to Toil, in memory of the loading and unloading of goods that once filled this site. As the slow movement of each pipe beam reaches the end of a beat, a drop of water is emitted from its top. Nearby, an aviary housing two white doves juts out of the park, bringing light to an underground assemblage.

Across Viale Umbria, in a Garden of Sounds, the park infiltrates the urban area. Within the garden is a seasonal children's zoo whose animals require a variety of cages and enclosures (the goat, the chicken, the cow, etc.). Other little programs are implied by the titles of the various areas: The

See-Saw, Fishing, The Picnic, The Water-Chute, The Sleigh, La Commedia Italiana, The Octopus, Hunting, Fireworks, Bocci Ball.

To the south of the site is a large public Botanical Garden with glass-roofed forms in a sprouting diversity parallel to the vegetation within. Over the sloping earthen floor of the interior are areas for experimental botany, checker and chess tables, and meeting tables. These are scattered throughout the green density of the vegetation. On the ground of the eastern portion is a darkened hall containing a cinema that dissects its interior. The public is exposed to back-projection on constructed objects, multiple separation, and other cinematic experiments.

Bounding the Botanical Garden is a large public fountain that is negotiated via stone steps and passages interwoven with cascades of water. The fountain opens onto a long basin for aquatic activities and barge-borne theatrical events. At the edge of this opening is a hotel for unhappy lovers. The plan has no interior corridors, setting the rooms of the hotel back-to-back. One large glass corridor belts the building. At the top is a crooked café-

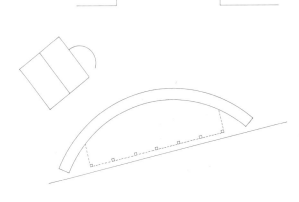

lounge and a wiry truss containing a footbridge to a suspended chapel. On the northeast portion of the site, a water channel is flanked by rudimentary housing for the homeless. Nearby, a public gymnasium is organized in a strip interwoven with spectator areas. To the west is a school of the humanities. Its central block of lecture rooms is banded by study room towers; visiting professors live in the upper portions. From the main building, a walkway connects to two wedge-shaped interrelated workshop-studios. To the west, a ramp cycles through a two-part correlating facility, leading upward into spaces more and more remote, arriving at a mechanical rooftop simulating teleological suspension.

Near Via F. Rezzonico is a sanctuary of the muses filled with ancient stone fragments. A modern cinema is inserted from the east. The public can move back and forth from celluloid simulation to stone materiality.

The new subway station opens to the west onto an elongated gap. Here the visitor passes through several activities, rising through an elliptical passage to the Garden of Sounds. Bureaucratic and

105

administrative activities (formless and always in flux) are given specific urban character in a thin tower, a four-sided pentagon, a double-flux slab (whose section can be altered), and large galleries along the water basin. The three lobbies of these work areas are connected by a central neck-shaped space.

Across Viale Muguello, to the east, larger programs fit into the existing city fabric. The airport connection station sits here; adjacent is the bus garage, housed below a public arena and velodrome.

Of these specific ideas, several might be realized, and yet the overall strategy and intention depends on none of them. They serve only as examples for the figure in the landscape of this city for which the unknown is a source of optimism. To affirm the joy of the present, to find lines of escape, to subvert an overall urban plan from within—via architecture—is part of projecting an open future as a source of freedom.

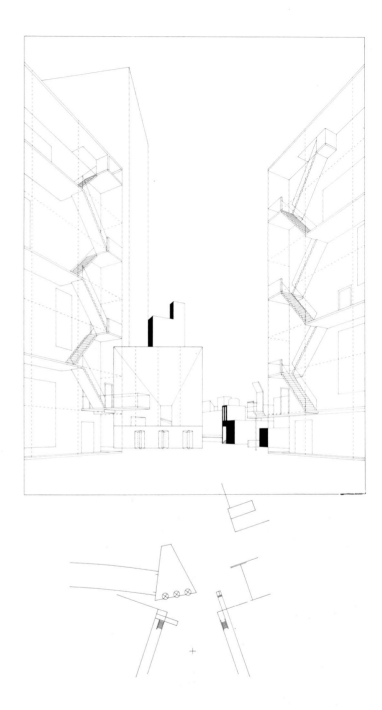

Above: Water basin, amphitheater and jack-up rig.
Left: Subway station.
Far left: View from four-sided pentagon.

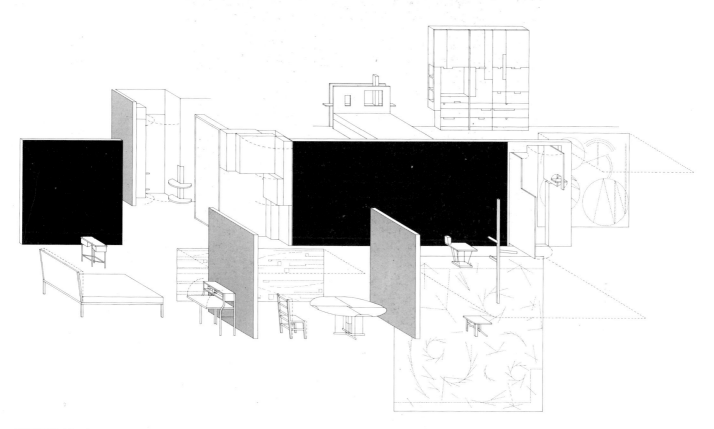

MUSEUM OF MODERN ART TOWER New York, New York 1986.

The interior renovation and design of fixtures and furniture began with a simple concept arrived at during the first encounter with the Manhattan site. The apartment tower rises directly up from its lot line, intensifying the experience of the Manhattan grid. Standing in the front corner window, the N-S and E-W geometry of the urban perspectives outside are particularly emphasized by the vanishing point in the Z (vertical) dimension. (From here the tower appears to be leaning over 53rd Street.)

This experience inspired the organization of all the elements in the apartment according to a lyrical illumination of the X, Y, and Z directions.

Plaster walls in the X direction are charcoal black integral color, while plaster walls in the Y direction are yellow. The Z dimension is emphasized in a long narrow corner lamp at the entry, in an intersected pole lamp near the main corner window, and in linear verticals in the furniture. Three wool carpets are fabricated for the apartment, one based on the X, one on the Y, and one on the Z dimension. Furniture specially designed for the apartment includes a dining table in which the X Y Z dimension is emphasized at its steel center while its edges are vaguely free form.

The elements present the original idea in a variety of ways—literal, poetic, systematic, intuitive. Seen together they do not become a collection of more or less equivalent examples; the differences in means prevent this. Their association is less didactic and more mysterious; the elements serve to form a ground for each other. Only in this indirect way does the original X Y Z idea prepare a relation between the parts.

This relation is spatial. That which is the object in one position is the reference in another. Their common result is a kind of suspension—a consequence of the suspended site, the vertiginous view.

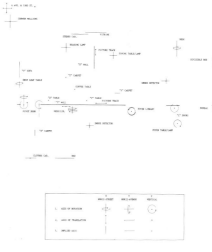

XYZ Diagram.

Left: View into dining room.
Below left: Corner shelf with interlocking door.
Below: Soap dish.

111

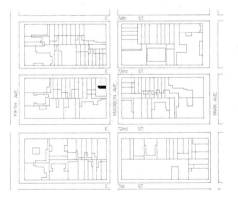

GIADA SHOWROOM New York, New York 1987.
The site is on a busy section of Madison Avenue, midblock between 72nd and 73rd Streets. The absolutely compressed condition of the 14' x 30' shop is situated with a large building above bearing down with more than gravitational force; economic pressure and time pressure together act like an invisible vise grip pressing the space in a psychological densification. The idea was to express the compression on the exterior and relieve it on the interior. All proportions are organized according to a logarithmic spiral of relations to the section.

On the exterior, cast glass, 3" slab glass, and brass plates express densification. The brass plates that contain and define the front are acid-etched to a dull red with flat-head and round-head screws spaced according to conceptual pressure. Bulging and bending shapes are heavy in contrast to interior elements.

Interior materials, bronze wire screen, brass mesh, and spun aluminum, express the light-weight. An 8" void below a "floating" terrazzo floor in cloud-like, hand-sprinkled terrazzo has pockets and trap doors opening up for various exhibit devices. When the wire skeleton mannequins with their cast glass shoulders are moved from pocket to pocket, the spaces below are being activated as anti-compression devices. Light ash doors at the changing rooms turn inside-out when not in use, giving their interior volumes back to the overall space.

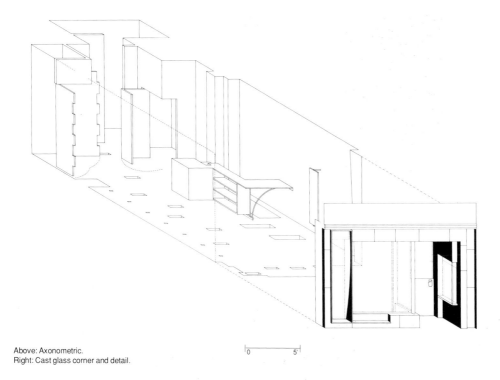

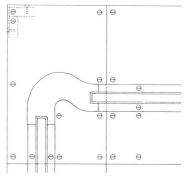

Above: Axonometric.
Right: Cast glass corner and detail.

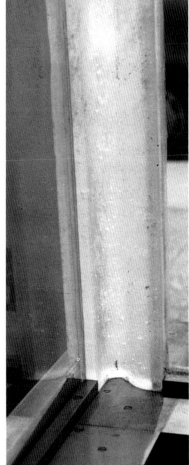

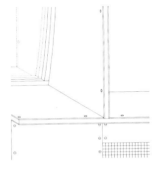

Right: Details showing glass in compression.
Below: Shelves of metal mail in tension;
door handle in peeled-away brass.

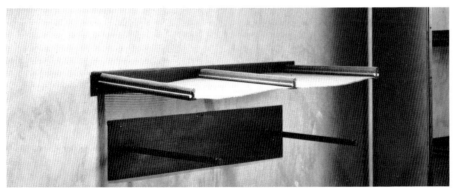

← SITE

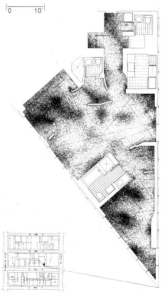

0   10'

METROPOLITAN TOWER APARTMENT New York, New York 1987–88. In the gridded city of Manhattan, ruthless economic forces have inserted a tall, sharp-pointed wedge of glass mid-block between 57th and 56th Streets. The point that rises up from the street edge becomes the crucial character of the interior, its shrill angle of 40° analogous to a shrill sound high in pitch (high in elevation).

The interior design is an intensification of this event or condition rather than a criticism or negation. No apparent traditional domesticity, no static rectilinearity or symmetry should attempt to reverse the direction already taken. Rather, what has started can take a more lyrical tone, increasing its non-rectilinearity and indeterminacy. A free floating spatial tilting is characterized by the 4° tilt of walls that accompany the acute angle of the existing plan. A floating cloud-like black and white terrazzo floor underlies the new free-form walls. The slight folds in the curved walls are like the folds in a paper airplane. In a range of sandblasted glass fixtures, interior night-lighting is diffused and indeterminant. An ultra-light curved wall fragment constructed in basswood and airplane silk is a kind of "Icaran wing" dividing the sleeping (dreams) area from the conscious area. Carpets are drawn from an intuited version of a piece of music, "Landscapes of the Mind," based on a painting by Georgia O'Keefe, "Sky Above Clouds." A floating cloud-like habitat striving for immateriality, this dwelling is in the evaporative dream state above the metropolis.

Above: Airplane silk and wood screen.
Left: Cast glass light.

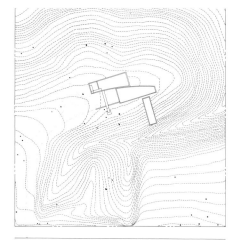

SHAKER BOULEVARD

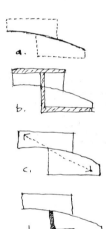

CLEVELAND HOUSE Cleveland, Ohio 1988.

A thickly wooded site east of Cleveland characterized by ravines and steep grades is the site for a house for a lawyer and his wife, a painter. Large open spaces and a vertical emphasis were requested, along with a three car garage. The house has a multi-level section shifted along a curve, which coincides with the central ravine on the site. A series of conditions erase the dialectic nature of the house's double-form:

a) The double form is displaced along the entrance plane of the house. Distinct from the other elevations, this blackened plane makes a "front" on the inside and the outside, north and south.

b) A "skywalk" suspended from the facade traverses both halves of the house, joining them in a continuous steel deck view of the trees.

c) Diagonal views of interior space, 100' in length, join both halves of the house.

d) Sleepwalk passage: above the "skywalk," a blind passage leads from the mezzanine to a roof terrace. This passage was inspired by C. Brockden Brown's novel, *Memoirs of a Sleep Walker*, published in 1879. The novel is based on his unpublished work *Sky Walk* (a corruption of "skiwakkee," the name given to the Delaware Indians, who were later driven into Ohio). Sleepwalking and a cave are metaphors Brown uses for subconsciousness. The novel revolves on dualities, coupling, intertwining, etc. Here the psycho-symbolic program of sleepwalking finds an architectural equivalent.

Cleveland's steel industries are employed in the steel construction. Varying automotive channel sections are rolled straight and spaced at 8' on center along the "skywalk." The remaining structure is plywood reinforced metal studs, steel-suspended walks, and steel windows.

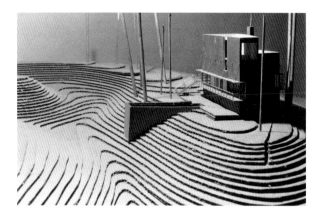

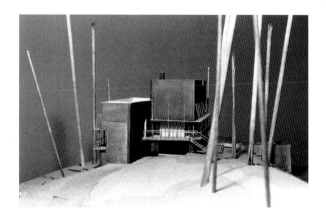

Basement:
1. Exercise area.
2. Guest bedroom.
3. Three car garage.
4. Pool.

First floor:
1. Entry.
2. Foyer.
3. Living.
4. Dining.
5. Sky walk.

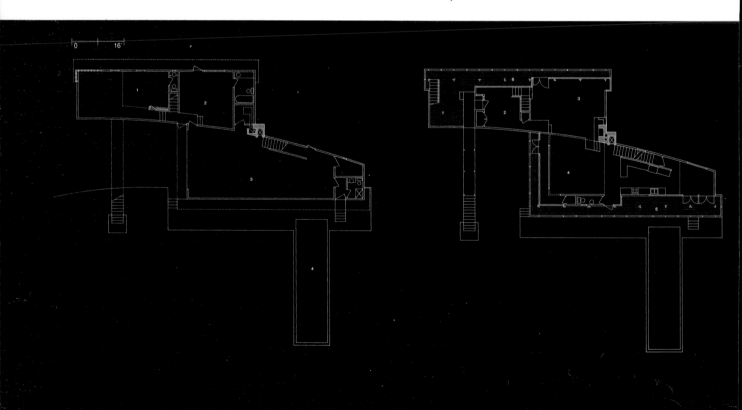

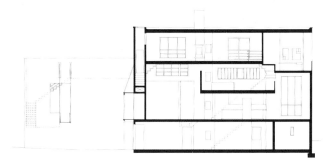

Third floor:
1. Roof terrace.
2. Master bedroom.
3. Sleepwalk passage.

Second floor:
1. Library.

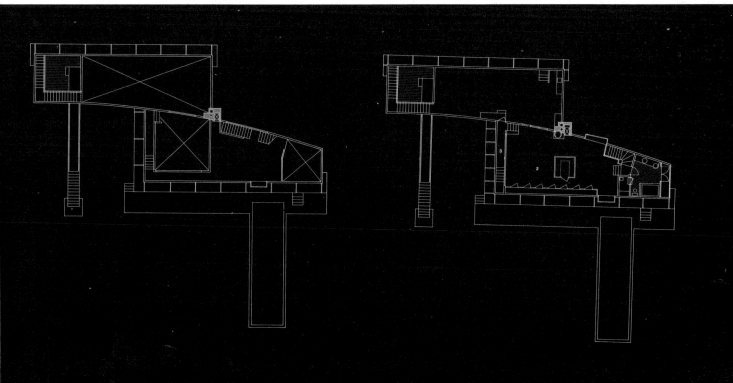

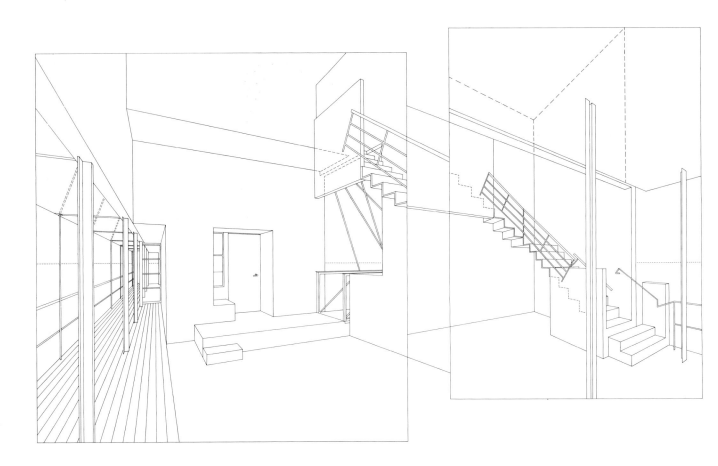

" . . . Passage into new forms, over-leaping the bars of time
and space, reversal of the laws of inanimate and intelligent
existence had been mine to perform and witness."
—Charles Brockden Brown
Edgar Huntly, or, Memoirs of a Sleepwalker

NIGHT | DAY

OXNARD HOUSE Oxnard, California 1988. A narrow sand lot in a row of similar lots near the Pacific Ocean is the site for a weekend house for a couple with two children and two cars. A view to the ocean is possible on the southwest corner of the lot at a ten foot elevation.

Space and light are taken as the materials of architectural expression, due to the necessary economy of construction and the qualities of California light. Interlocking solids define interlocking interior spaces in plan, and section, modulated by the passing arc of the sun. In the north, "L" are night functions, in the south, day functions. The entry stair is in a "volume of shadows" at the center of the plan—a void open to the sky. Uninterrupted walls allow the sun to emphasize wall mass and define interior spaces by washes of sunlight.

Construction is of stained concrete block grouted solid with steel reinforcement. The north solid has a black stained north elevation; the south, a white stained elevation. Between the interlocking forms are colors with their complimentary colors painted on the opposing wall (north = blue, south = yellow). Windows are steel framed with obscure-glass sections sandblasted or back-painted with white paint. The roof is rubber membrane with a walking deck in lightweight concrete pavers.

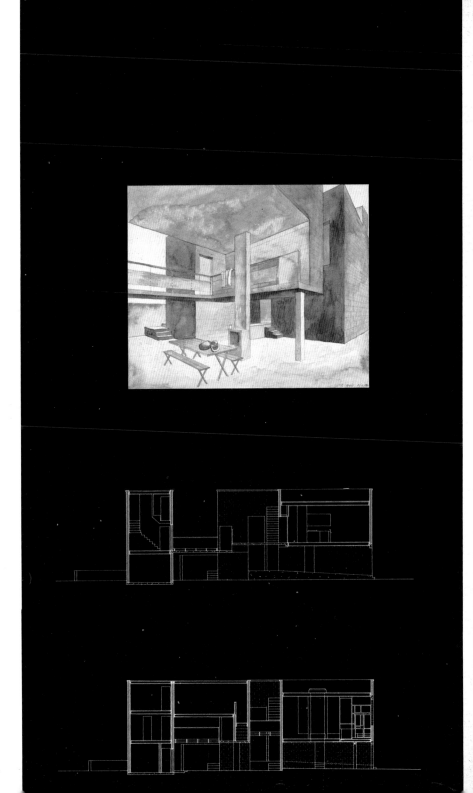

Section A-A.

Section B-B.

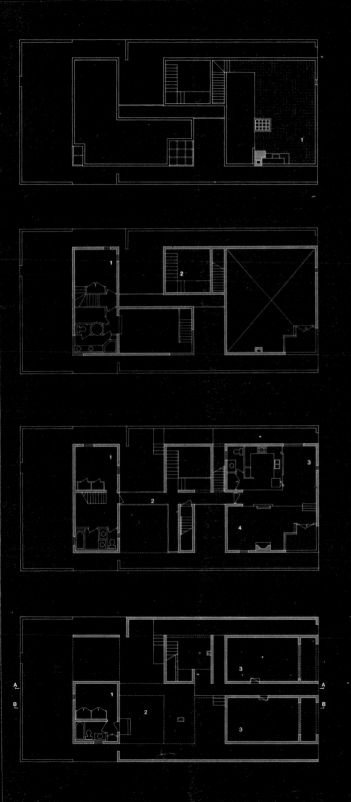

Fourth Floor:
1. Roof terrace.

Third Floor:
1. Bedroom.
2. Entry (volume of shadows).

Second Floor:
1. Bedroom.
2. Walkway.
3. Dining room.
4. Living room.

First Floor:
1. Bedroom.
2. Sand court.
3. Garage.

BERLIN LIBRARY COMPETITION Berlin, West Germany, 1988.

This project is a competition entry for an addition to the Amerika Gedenk Bibliothek in Berlin and surrounding area.

The design extends the philosophical position of the open stack—the unobstructed meeting of the reader and the book—by organizing the offerings along a browsing circuit. The circuit is a public path looping the building, presenting the collection of the entire library. The library stacks are developed as furniture, giving different characteristics to areas of the open plan. The concept of a browsing circuit is given memorable variety by these different stack arrangements.

The circuit forms a slipped ring bracketing the original building. The extension holds the original building in space without overpowering or deferring to it. Proportions of all major architectural elements, including interior and exterior spaces and structural grid, are determined by a single series (1:1.618) based on the height of the existing building.

The importance of the site within the city plan is expressed by making the library a major urban element, analogous to a city gate. The north face of the library addition defines the south edge of the new Blücherplatz. Additional buildings to the east and west, containing public programs, complete the definition of space. A clearly defined park to the east and west strengthens the connection to the Holy Cross Church. The tower offers a public observation point—a lens focused on the city—and contains the children's library. Suspended over Berlin, the library elevates children to caretakers of the city. It has sloped floors for reading while lying down. The structure is a lattice truss sheathed in sandblasted glass with vision panels.

The main structure is an exposed concrete frame with glass curtain walls of sandblasted white, amber, and blue glass set off by areas of lead or stainless-steel covered panels. Under the gray skies of Berlin, the effects of east and west light in the library will be highly varied according to the sandblasted lines and mullion patterns in the curtain walls. For the interior, careful attention has been given to acoustics to assure silence, while natural materials and subdued colors have been selected for their contributions to a serene and reflective mood.

Urban diagram.

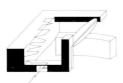

Circuit diagram.

Variety of stacks.

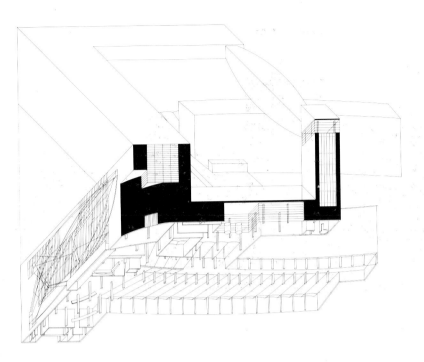

Above: Worm's eye axonometric.
Top: Existing building.
Middle: Existing site.
Bottom: Project site plan.

Floor III:
1. Art and Music Department.
2. Children's Library office.
3. "Circuit" moving ramp.

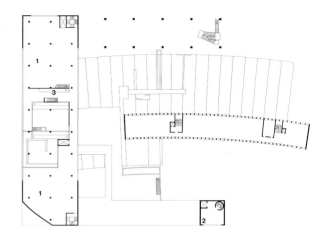

0   30m

Floor II:
1. Reference, below.
2. Reading terrace.
3. Commemorative objects.
4. Court, below.
5. Café terrace.
6. Staff lounge.
7. Café, below.
8. Staff lunchroom.
9. Stair to exhibition area.
10. Stair to periodicals.
11. "Circuit" moving ramp.
12. Existing building's offices.

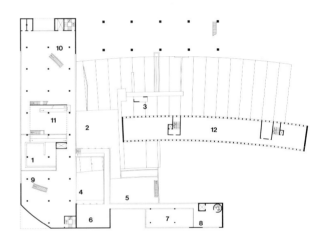

Main Floor:
1. Main entrance.
2. Café.
3. Coat room.
4. Meeting room.
5. Court, below.
6. Exhibition area.
7. Humanities Department
(existing building).
8. Reference area.
9. Study mezzanine.
10. Service entrance.
11. Stair to parking under plaza.
12. Elevator to Children's Library.
13. Paranoid Fire Stair.

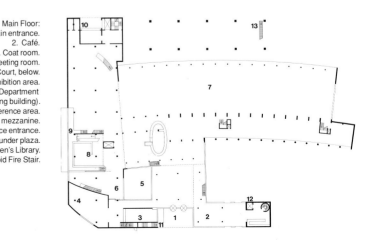

Floor VI:
1. Natural Sciences Department.
2. Terrace.
3. Berlin collection.
4. Children's Library.
5. Mezzanine.
6. Observation room, above.
7. Bypass.
8. Stair to roof garden.
9. "Circuit" moving ramp.

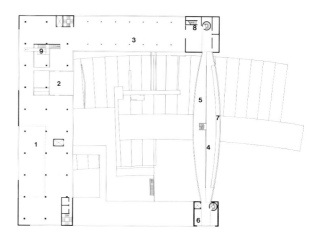

Floor V:
1. Social Sciences Department II.
2. Library Technical Services.
3. Children's Library work space.
4. "Circuit" moving ramp.

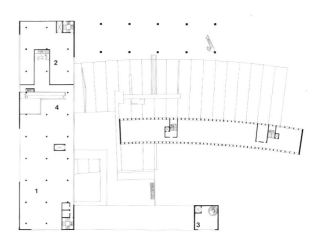

Floor IV:
1. Social Sciences Department I.
2. Computer Department.
3. Children's Library office.
4. "Circuit" moving ramp.

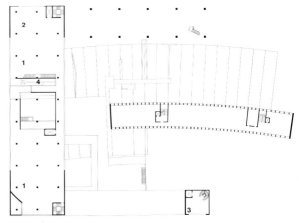

131

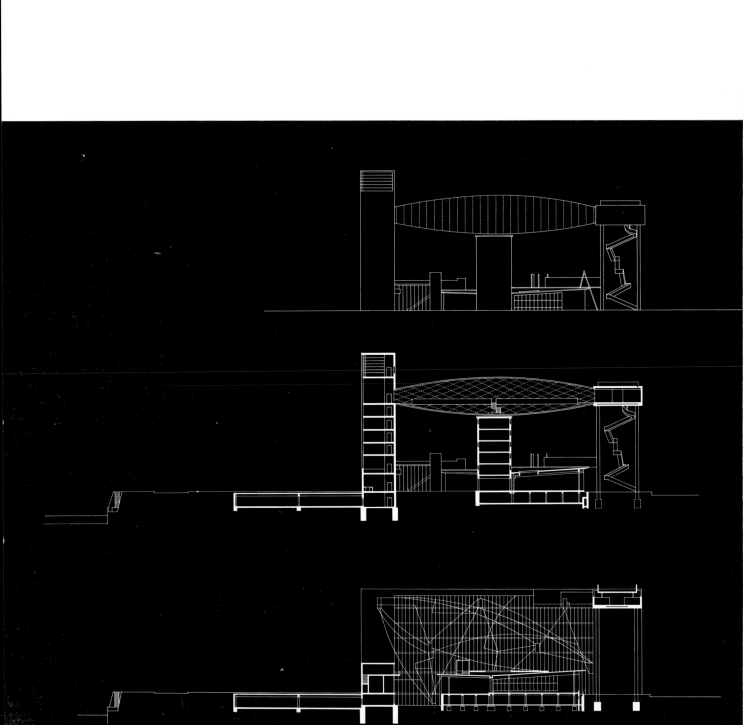

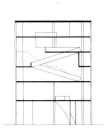

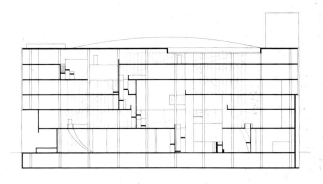

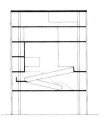

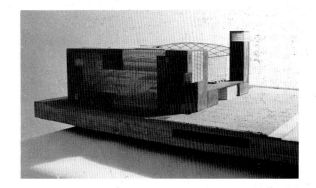

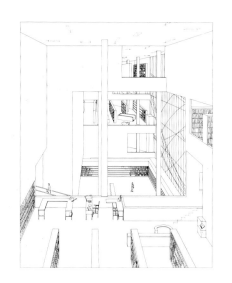

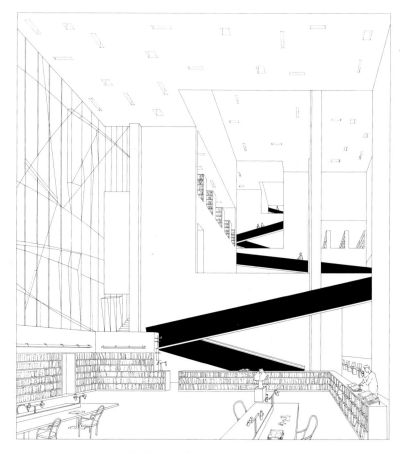

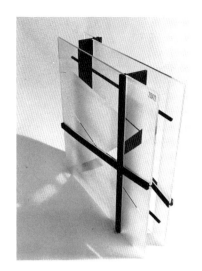

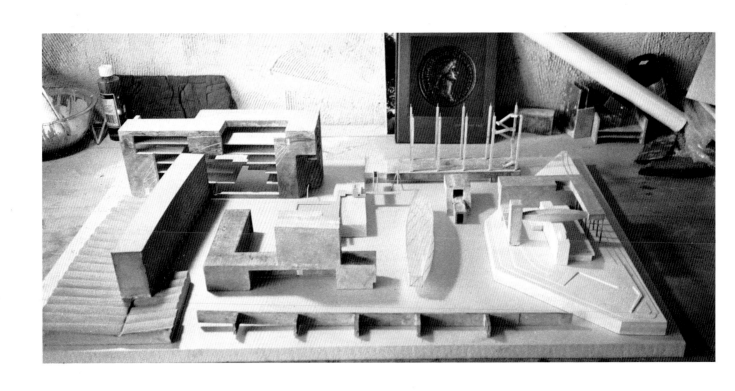

CHRONOLOGICAL LIST OF SELECTED WORKS

Date	Project	Collaborators/Assistants
1975	**Manila Housing**	James Tanner John Cropper
1976	**Sokolov Retreat**	
1976	**St. Paul Capital Competition**	James Tanner William Zimmerman
1977	**Gymnasium Bridge**	
1978	**Telescope House**	Joseph Fenton
1978	**Millville Courtyard**	Joseph Fenton
1977–78	**Minimum Houses**	
1979	**Les Halles Competition**	Joseph Fenton Ron Stiener Stuart Diston
1979–82	**Bridge of Houses**	Mark Janson Joseph Fenton Suzanne Powadiuk James Rosen
1980	**Metz House**	Joseph Fenton Mark Janson James Rosen Paolo Iacucci Melita Prieto
1980–81	**Pool House and Sculpture Studio**	Mark Janson James Rosen
1982–83	**Guardian Safe Depository**	Joseph Fenton Mark Janson
1982–83	**Van Zandt House**	Joseph Fenton Mark Janson Peter Shinoda Charles Anderson
1982–83	**Cohen Apartment**	Mark Janson Joseph Fenton
1980–84	**Artisans' Housing**	Mark Janson David Kessler Paola Iacucci
1984	**Ocean Front House, Leucadia**	Mark Janson Peter Lynch Suzanne Powadiuk
1984–88	**Martha's Vineyard House**	Peter Lynch Ralph Nelson Peter Shinoda Stephen Cassell
1984–88	**Hybrid Building, Seaside**	Stephen Cassell Lorcan O'Herlihy Peter Lynch Richard Warner Philip Teft Laurie Beckerman
1986	**Pace Showroom**	Peter Shinoda Peter Lynch Paola Iacucci Donna Seftel Tom Van Den Bout
1986	**Milan Project**	Peter Lynch Jacob Allerdice Laurie Beckerman Meta Brunzema Stephen Cassell Gisue Hariri Mojgan Hariri Paola Iacucci James Leet Ralph Nelson Ron Peterson Darius Sollohub Lynnette Widder
1986	**MoMA Tower Apartment**	Peter Lynch Stephen Cassell Ralph Nelson
1987	**Giada Shop**	Peter Lynch Stephen Cassell Darius Sollohub
1987–88	**Metropolitan Tower Apartment**	Stephen Cassell Lorcan O'Herlihy Atsushi Aiba
1988	**Cleveland House**	Peter Lynch Lawrence Davis Kent Hikida Pier Copat Thomas Gardner Stephen Cassell
1988	**Oxnard House**	Lorcan O'Herlihy Richard Warner Peter Lynch Elizabeth Lerer Pier Copat Kent Hikida Thomas Gardner Patricia Bosch
1988	**Berlin AGB Library**	Peter Lynch Stephen Cassell Pier Copat Bryan Bell Friederike Grosspietshe Thomas Gardner

BIBLIOGRAPHY
PUBLISHED PROJECTS
1989
Wrede, Stuart, ed. *Emilio Ambasz/Steven Holl: Architecture,* The Museum of Modern Art exhibition catalogue, New York, February 1989.

1988
New York Architecture Vol. 1 New York Chapter AIA. 1988 Design Awards Program. 1988, pp. 11, 16–17, 51–52, 58–61.

Fischer, Thomas. "A Literary House." *Progressive Architecture,* December 1988, pp. 62–67.

Russell, James S. "Skin and Bones." *Architectural Record,* Mid-September 1988, pp. 122–127.

"House for Mr. and Mrs. B." *Utopica Two Architecture/Nature,* 1988, pp. 64–69.

Byron, Elizabeth S. "The Holl Truth." *House and Garden,* September 1988, pp. 184–191, 245.

"Architects Review Furniture: 7 Leading Architects Think About What Works, What Doesn't—And Why." *Architectural Digest,* August 1988, pp. 52, 56.

"The Conviction of This Project Is . . . ." *Off Ramp* (Sci-Arc Journal), 1988.

"Awards." *Occulus,* vol. 50, March 1988, pp. 6, 11.

"Three Projects." *A+U,* January 1988, pp. 39–58.

1987
"The Emerging Generation in USA: Steven Holl." *GA Houses Special 2,* 1987, pp. 92–97.

Guerrera, Giuseppe. "Stephen Holl." *New York Architects,* 1987, pp. 109–113.

"Le Citta Immaginate." *XVII Triennale Di Milano Catalogue* (Milan: Electa), 1987, pp. 292–295.

"Porta Vittoria Project Area." *Lotus International* #54, 1987, pp. 96–193.

Bethany, Marilyn. "What's Modern Now? Surprise Package." *New York Magazine,* 28 September 1987, pp. 64–67.

Stein, Karen D. "Portfolio: Steven Holl Architects." *Architectural Record,* September 1987, cover and pp. 90–101.

Di Giorgio, Manolo. "Una Piccola Galeria A Manhattan." *Domus,* June 1987, pp. 5–6.

"Showroom for the Pace Collection." *A+U,* May 1987, pp. 89–94.

"Steven Holl, Three Projects." *AA Files* #14, Spring 1987, pp. 18–24.

34th PA Awards: Citation—Hybrid Building. *Progressive Architecture,* January 1987, pp. 108–109.

1986
Nicolin, Pierluigi, ed. "Commercial Buildings with Residences." *Lotus International* #50, 1986, pp. 27–29.

Nicolin, Pierluigi, ed. "Bridge of Houses in Manhattan, Individual Characterizations, Urban Houses in N. America." *Lotus International* #44, 1986, pp. 41–50; projects and research.

McNair, Andrew. "40 Under 40." *Interiors,* September 1986, p. 175.

"Works: Stephen Holl." *A+U,* August 1986, pp. 59–74.

Smith, C. Ray. "Tale of 2 Interiors." *Unique Homes (City Living),* June/July 1986.

"New York Showroom." *Nikkei Architecture,* May 1986, pp. 82–87.

Gandee, Charles K. "Pace Maker." *Architectural Record,* April 1986, pp. 93–103.

Adams, Janet. "The Avant Garde Grows Up." *Blueprint* #35, March 1986, pp. 34–35, 38.

33rd PA Awards: Citation—Berkowitz House. *Progressive Architecture,* January 1986, pp. 104–106.

"Expressions: 5 New Design Stores." *New York Times,* 16 January 1986, Section C-1.

Bethany, Marilyn. "Setting the Pace." *New York Magazine,* January 1986, pp. 44–46.

1985
"Record Interiors, 1984." *Nikkei Architecture,* 1985, cover and pp. 179–184.

Bartos, A. "A Humanistic Approach to Building Design." *Esquire,* December 1985, p. 84.

"Modernism Takes a New Turn." *Home Decorating,* Fall 1985, pp. 30–35.

Davis, Douglas. *Newsweek,* 12 August 1985, p. 64.

"Cohen Apartment." *Occulus,* May 1985, p. 3.

Greenstreet, Bob. "Law: Who Really Owns Your Designs." *Progressive Architecture,* April 1985, p. 63.

1984
Gandee, Charles K. "Homework." *Architectural Record Interiors,* Fall 1984, pp. 156–163.

Philipps, Patricia C. "Stephen Holl at Facade Gallery." *Artforum,* October 1984, p. 93.

Giovannini, Joseph. "An Unbuilt House Sets Up a Quandary." *The New York Times,* 18 October 1984.

"Accent on Grandeur." *Newsweek,* 3 September 1984, pp. 70–71.

Regnier, Constance. "Ein Kuehnes Experiment Mit 3 Deimensionen." *Ambiente,* August 1984, cover and pp. 3, 118–127.

Bethany, Marilyn. "The Look of the 80s." *New York Magazine,* 16 April 1984, cover and pp. 54–56.

"Steven Holl." *'Architecture in Transition' Neue Architektur: Sieben Junge Architekten aus Amerika, Deutschland, England und Italien,* exhibition catalogue, April 1984, pp. 44–53.

31st PA Awards—Van Zandt Residence. *Progressive Architecture,* January 1984, pp. 102–103.

1983
"Deposito de Casas de Seguridad / Estudio de Escultura y Casa de Baños." *Arquitectura,* September/October 1983, pp. 66–68.

Viladas, Pilar. "Banca Rotunda." *Progressive Architecture,* September 1983, pp. 100–103.

Giovannini, Joseph. "Designers are Creating Etched Glass Renaissance." *The New York Times,* 11 August 1983, pp. C-1, C-10.

Filler, Martin. "A Poetry of Place." *House & Garden,* May 1983, pp. 78–81.

"Pont de Maisons: Projet pour Manhattan." *Architecture D'Aujord'hui,* February 1983, pp. 9–10.

1982
Iaccuci. "Projects: Poolhouse by Steven Holl." *Archetype,* vol. II, no. IV, Fall 1982, pp. 26–29.

Miller, Nory. "Braving the Elements." *Progressive Architecture,* July 1982, pp. 78–81.

"Neue Tendenzen in den USA: Steven Holl." *Werk, Bauen, & Wohnen,* May 1982, pp. 40–43.

"Works: Sculpture Studio by Steven Holl." *A+U,* April 1982, pp. 46–50.

"New Waves in American Architecture: 3." *GA Houses* #10, March 1982, pp. 128–137.

Weinstein, Edward. "Steven Holl: Hybrid Architect." *Arcade,* February/March 1982.

29th PA Awards—Metz House. *Progressive Architecture,* January 1982, pp. 152–155.

1981
"Three Projects." *A+U,* April 1981, pp. 73–84.

Miller, Nory. "Interventions: Good Fences." *Progressive Architecture,* February 1981, pp. 92–93.

1980
Emery, Marc. "Consultation Internationale sur le Quartier des Halles, Paris." *Architecture D'Aujord'hui,* April 1980, p. 7.

1979
Maroni, Angioli. "Tre Edifici." *New Americans,* 1979, p. 55.

Domus, December 1979, p. 7; Sokolov Project.

Archetype, vol. 1, no. 1, Spring 1979, pp. 29–30.

Battisti, Emilio. "Tre Giovano Architetti Americani." *Controspazio,* April 1979, pp. 49–53.

"Retreat for M. Sokolov." *A+U,* February 1979, p. 22.

1978
Selig, M. "Gymnasium-Bridge: Checkerboard Site Plan to Signal Hope and Despair." *The Harlem River Yards: Bridging a South Bronx Community Need,* 1978, pp. 6–8; study.

25th PA Awards: "Haunting Image by a Young Architect." *Progressive Architecture,* January 1978, p. 81.

Architecture of Self-Help Communities. January 1978, pp. 66–71.

1976

Baumeister, October 1976, cover.

"Prelude au Congres de Vancouver Habitat '76." *Architecture D'Aujord'hui*, no. 185, May/June 1976, pp. 90–91.

Wagner, Walter F. "International Design Competition for the Urban Environment of Developing Countries." *Architectural Record* 5, May 1976, pp. 136–139.

1973

Hilgenhurst, Ch. A. "Back from Niagara." *Architecture Plus*, April 1973, pp. 74–75.

EXHIBITIONS

The Museum of Modern Art, New York City February 9–April 4, 1989.

"Global Architecture: Houses." GA Gallery, Tokyo, Japan, 1987.

"House/Housing." John Nichols Gallery, New York City, October–November, 1987.

"New York Architects." Gullans International, New York City, 1987.

XVII Triennale of Milan, Urban Section. Milan, Italy, 1987.

"What Could Have Been: Unbuilt Architecture of the '80's." USA traveling exhibit, 1986–89.

"High Styles." American Design (2 pieces), Whitney Museum, New York City, 1985.

"Anchorage." One man show, Princeton School of Architecture, Princeton, New Jersey, Spring 1985.

"Architecture in Transition." Berlin, Germany, October 1984.

"Cultural Connection and Modernity." One man show, Facade Gallery, New York City, June 1984.

"Architecture in Transition." Pfalzgalerie Kaiserlautern, Germany, May 1984.

"Metamanhattan." Whitney Museum Downtown, New York City, January 1984.

"Bridge of Houses." White Columns Gallery, New York City, September 1982.

"Bridges." One man show, Architettura Arte Moderna, Rome, December 1981.

"Window, Room, Furniture." Group show, Cooper Union, New York City, December 1981.

"Concept Drawings." Group show, Erica Williams/Johnson Gallery, Seattle, November 1981.

"Young Architects." Yale School of Architecture Gallery, New Haven, January–February 1980.

Group Show, Rizzoli Gallery, New York City, January 1980.

"Young American Architects." Rome, August 1979 (Traveled to Pisa, Florence, Bologna).

"Drawings—Steven Holl." William Stout Architectural Books, San Francisco, March 1978.

"Steven Holl, Projects." University of Washington School of Architecture, Seattle, 1978.

PUBLISHED WRITINGS

Anchoring. Princeton Architectural Press, New York, February 1989.

"Within the City: Phenomena of Relations." *Design Quarterly*, no. 139, M. Friedman, ed., Walker Art Center, Minneapolis, Spring 1988, entire issue.

"Teeter Totter Principles." *Perspecta 21: The Yale Architectural Journal*, New Haven, 1984, pp. 30–51.

"Foundations: American House Types." *Precis IV*, Columbia University, New York, 1983, pp. 36–37; excerpt from *Pamphlet Architecture #9.*

Pamphlet Architecture #9: Urban and Rural House Types, New York, 1982.

"The Anatomy of a Skyscraper." *Cities—The Forces that Shape Them,* Liza Taylor, ed., Cooper-Hewitt Museum, New York, 1982, pp. 68–69.

"Conversation with Alberto Sartoris." *Archetype,* San Francisco, Fall 1982.

Pamphlet Architecture #7: Bridge of Houses, New York, 1981.

Pamphlet Architecture #5: The Alphabetical City, New York, 1980.

"USSR in the USA." *Skyline,* New York, May 1979.

"The Desert De Retz." *Student Quarterly,* Syracuse School of Architecture, Syracuse, December 1978.

"Review of Blue Mountain Conference." *Skyline,* New York, November 1978.

Pamphlet Architecture #1: Bridges, New York, 1977.

"A New Wave of European Architecture." *A+U,* Tokyo, Japan, August 1977.

PHOTO CREDITS

G. Carlo Argan, *Libera*. Rome: Editalia, 1975, p.11.

Adam Bartos, pp. 54-57.

Richard Bryant, pp. 118t, 119.

Stephen Cassell, pp. 74, 77t, 79tr.

Jim Daddio, pp. 50r, 51.

Mark C. Darley, pp. 110, 111t, 112, 113, 115.

Narayan R. Gokhale, *Hailstorms and Hailstone Growth*. Albany: State University of New York Press, 1975, p. 12.

Horst Janus. *Nature as Architect*. New York: Frederick Ungar Publishing Co., p. 12.

Beckett Logan, p. 531.

Paul Warchol, pp. 62-64, 77b, 79tl, 90, 92-95, 108, 111b, 116, 117tl, 118b.

Susan Wides, pp. 85, 96, 103-4, 107.

Special thanks to Paul Warchol, National Reprographics, and Kennedy Photo Works.